Cambridge Elements ≡

Elements in Psychology and Culture
edited by
Kenneth D. Keith
University of San Diego

THE CONTINUING GROWTH OF CROSS-CULTURAL PSYCHOLOGY

A First-Person Annotated Chronology

Walter J. Lonner, Professor Emeritus
Western Washington University

CAMBRIDGE
UNIVERSITY PRESS

CAMBRIDGE
UNIVERSITY PRESS

University Printing House, Cambridge CB2 8BS, United Kingdom

One Liberty Plaza, 20th Floor, New York, NY 10006, USA

477 Williamstown Road, Port Melbourne, VIC 3207, Australia

314–321, 3rd Floor, Plot 3, Splendor Forum, Jasola District Centre,
New Delhi – 110025, India

79 Anson Road, #06–04/06, Singapore 079906

Cambridge University Press is part of the University of Cambridge.

It furthers the University's mission by disseminating knowledge in the pursuit of
education, learning, and research at the highest international levels of excellence.

www.cambridge.org
Information on this title: www.cambridge.org/9781108461726
DOI: 10.1017/9781108562294

First published 2018

A catalogue record for this publication is available from the British Library.

ISBN 978-1-108-46172-6 Paperback
ISSN 2515-3943 (online)
ISSN 2515-3986 (print)

Cambridge Elements ⚏

The Continuing Growth of Cross-Cultural Psychology

Walter J. Lonner

Abstract: *Written largely in a personal manner, this Element summarizes many noteworthy developments in cross-cultural psychology during the past half-century. The essence of this chronology is the author's deep involvement with the* Journal of Cross-Cultural Psychology *(JCCP) and the International Association for Cross-Cultural Psychology (IACCP). It presents developments in a decade-by-decade format. This approach allows brief discussion of high points in each decade, such as significant conferences and books, as well as commentaries about other culture-oriented perspectives in psychology, such as cultural psychology, indigenous psychology, and psychological anthropology. The topics covered include summaries of all international IACCP conferences, the* Online Readings in Psychology and Culture *(ORPC), the IACCP Archives, and the assessment of introductory psychology texts and their cultural content. Overviews of key elements in culture-centered methodology in psychology and the teaching of culture-oriented psychology conclude the presentation.*

Keywords: *Culture, Psychology, Cross-Cultural*

ISBNs: *9781108461726 (PB) 9781108562294 (OC)*

ISSNs: *2515–3943 (online) 2515–3986 (print)*

1 Introduction

In September 1969 George A. Miller delivered his presidential address to the American Psychological Association (APA).

The title was "Psychology as a Means of Promoting Human Welfare." He began his talk with a riveting paragraph:

> The most urgent problems of our world today are the problems we have made for ourselves. They have not been caused by some heedless malicious inanimate Nature, nor have they been imposed on us as punishment by the will of God. They are human problems whose solutions will require us to change our behavior and our social institutions.   (Miller, 1969, p. 1063)

In view of the lengthening list of human-made tragedies during the past half-century – the Viet Nam War, horrific slaughters in Africa, 9/11, terrorism, mass shootings of innocent people, the humanitarian crisis in Syria, and widespread home-lessness, among others – Miller's address, delivered nearly half a century ago, continues to express a sense of compassionate urgency. It provided a fitting and appropriate end to a decade – the tumultuous 1960s – that finally witnessed the insertion of culture into the psychological equation. Miller delivered his talk when I was beginning my first full year as a tenure-track assis-tant professor and also just six months from my being the midwife in inaugurating the *Journal of Cross-Cultural Psychology*, a periodical that has absorbed my attention for half a century. Three years later, in 1972, the IACCP was formed, and other efforts along the same lines were soon to follow. I was eager to contribute to the psychological perspec-tive that Miller described. To have such a renowned psycholo-gist say such things at a critical period in the development of cross-cultural psychology was, and remains, uplifting.

As I contend in the following pages, from the mid-1960s and especially the 1970s, the concept of culture helped to alter the direction and content of psychology to such an extent that it is now on course to become a transformed and globalized discipline. I have not read all of the addresses given by APA presidents throughout the association's history (who has?), but surely Miller's was the first, or at least among the first, to recognize the importance of culture to the discipline. He wrote:

One of the most basic ideas in all the social sciences is the concept of culture. Social anthropologists have developed a conception of culture as an organic whole, in which each particular value, practice, or assumption must be understood in the context of the total system. They tell terrible tales about the consequences of introducing Western reforms into aboriginal cultures without understanding the social equilibria that would be upset.   (p. 1071)

For years I have thought of Miller's address as his admonishing gift to "give psychology away" for the benefit of all mankind. In that context, I believe that the most important service culture-oriented psychologists can "give away" to the world is to "study all that is human," which was a guiding principle, and its mantra, when I was preparing the JCCP for its March 1970 inauguration. Knowledge is power. Through their research and scholarship, psychologists who focus on global issues, culture-comparative topics, culture-comparative and/or culturally intensive topics, and other contributions that focus on psychology and culture can "give away" their ever-accumulating knowledge of how culture affects all branches of psychology and, therefore, all explanations of similarities as well as differences in thought and behavior.

I believe and hope that the Elements series will be guided by these principles and overriding philosophy. In the following pages I intend to explain in elementary terms the various ways that cross-cultural psychology offers its brand of psychology for the betterment of the entire planet and its growing population.

2 Culture and Psychology: A Long Courtship and Brief History

The concept of human culture (and related terms such as "ethnicity" and "diversity," and sometimes, the controversial concept of race) has been a mainstay in the social and behavioral sciences for many decades, and arguably for many centuries. It is common knowledge that some academic orientations have thrived on the term, with cultural anthropology being a prime and obvious example. But this volume is not about the lengthy, though opaque, history of the culture concept in various scholarly disciplines. Nor is it directly concerned with details about culture and cognition, perception, personality, brain structure and function, or any of the other psychological specialties, for there are plenty of references to them in the following pages and the many books and journal articles in the references. Rather, this brief treatise is primarily part of what I hope will be an introduction to other Elements manuscripts, not yet written or conceived, about how the myriad of human cultures – real, palpable, and indispensable social entities – have been the focus in the discipline of psychology.

So-called mainstream psychology has largely been shaped by the overwhelming productivity of Western psychology, led by the United States and its territorial and linguistic extensions (Arnett, 2008). Heavily influenced by early European pioneers, the popular discipline has been a real force in the development of theories, the promulgation of millions of research projects, and creative applications in every walk of life. In short, psychology has established itself as a major dynamic and viable discipline with a very bright future. Its future will always be brighter if it incorporates culture in all of its efforts and gradually reaches the point where global psychology is finally achieved. That goal and how it may be reached has been alive and well for many years and has become a hot topic (e.g., Berry, 2013; Keith, 2018; Lonner, Keith, & Matsumoto, in press).

2.1 A Focus on Cross-Cultural Psychology

This Element summarizes the recent history and essence of one important aspect of the colorful history of psychology. It mainly focuses on *cross-cultural psychology*, which is a comparative enterprise that demands unique methods. It also touches on other culture-oriented perspectives in psychology that nicely complement the comparative element generally espoused by cross-cultural psychology. This Element does not, however, pretentiously inject culture into the discipline for the first time. Far from it. The concept of culture, or the "other," as already noted, has been employed throughout its history, and rightly so. But certain quite clear events and initiatives during the past half-century, markedly starting to coalesce in the 1960s, were pivotal. These events and activities contributed to the institutionalization of cross-cultural psychology as well as like-minded efforts such as cultural psychology, indigenous psychology, multiculturalism, and more (see Lonner et al., in press). Contemporary psychology is now the beneficiary of multiple culture-oriented perspectives. The remainder of this Element gives an account – often in the first person – of its development. I want to thank Ken Keith for inviting me to write this introductory piece for the forthcoming papers he will solicit and edit. As the lead entry for the Elements series, it will help, I hope, to stimulate a parade of Elements that contribute to an area of inquiry meriting the continued attention of present scholars and the interest of future contributors to the worldwide growth of this facet of the discipline of psychology.

2.2 An Expansion of the Intent of This Element

Imagine a timeline beginning on your left and progressing to your right (for the clock and Gregorian calendar tell us that time moves in that direction). On the far left ("Way Back When") were faint rumblings by scholars who "broke out of the box" and started to discover and explore aspects of human functioning in faraway lands that had been generally neglected for centuries. Some distance to the right on the timeline is the present state of such thinking, and even further to the right are the things waiting to be discovered and explored. Because this Element is a *chronology*, or somewhat of a timeline of cross-cultural psychology, the main focus is on the continuing growth of this particular orientation in the discipline. As such, it necessarily deals with many of the whens, whys, whos, wheres, and hows of culture's influence on psychological research, theory, and applications.

These constituent components comprise a story – a story that will undoubtedly vary, depending on who is telling it, for historical treatments of any movement in any discipline can be quite subjective. History is in the eye of the beholder. I am but one of numerous psychologists who have had lengthy, career-long experiences with the area that is now, in its modern form, more than half a century old. Any culture-oriented psychologist whose career in the discipline has spanned four decades or more has a compelling story to tell about "the beginnings." My career has been richly nourished by colleagues such as John Berry, Harry Triandis, Ype Poortinga, Geert Hofstede, and virtually all who played important roles in the development of the *Journal of Cross-Cultural Psychology* and, more lately, the *Online Readings in Psychology and Culture*. Recently deceased scholars such as Ernest Boesch (see Lonner & Hayes, 2007), Çiğdem Kağıtçıbaşı, the inimitable Gustav Jahoda, the energetic Kwok Leung, and the insightful Paul Pedersen made indelible contributions and in the process created many stories. Some of these scholars were among those who were briefly featured in a 1997 book edited by Michael Bond that was recently reprinted (Bond, 2015). Ruth Munroe, who died in 1996, was a close friend and telephone buddy before the Internet takeover. I miss her wisdom tinted by clever humor. I could go on and on about a close network of thoughtful people. Fortunately, the lives of many dozens of scholars are briefly profiled in Ken Keith's (2013) three-volume *Encyclopedia of Cross-Cultural Psychology*. In a multitude of ways, these people and many more made my career invigorating and challenging. They were witnesses of and contributors to the various branches of culture-oriented psychology. Readers of these profiles will be richly rewarded by learning more about them.

Thus, my story is merely one of many stories that could be, and have been, told and therefore has my own imprint. And rather than simply providing a chronological list of major developments over the years, I try here to add some color and texture to my journey of more than half a century. At the same time, I strive for accuracy with respect to activities, events, and the contributions made by many of the people who have been involved in the development of cross-cultural psychology.

2.3 A Final Introductory Note

The main target audience for this Element includes advanced undergraduates, graduate students, and freshly minted academic psychologists who wish to know more about cross-cultural psychology. Seasoned psychologists who may read this will likely be familiar with other culture-oriented perspectives, and may want to introduce them to their students as well. They may also become motivated to write an Element that fits the purpose of the Psychology and Culture series.

3 Any Road Has to Begin Somewhere, Doesn't It?

A large majority of "old timers" whose dedicated involvement in cross-cultural psychology spans more than four decades did not choose to be cross-cultural psychologists at the onset of their careers. Many of those in the current generation of cross-cultural psychologists – the "baby boomers" and "millennials" and members of "Generation X" as they are called in the United States – were likely taught by psychologists who themselves were the academic offspring of seasoned cross-culturalists. Those in this third generation of cross-cultural psychologists have benefited from a virtual avalanche of books, monographs, workshops, and conference presentations that helped shape the current status of culture-oriented psychology. By stark contrast, life circumstances, unexpected opportunities, happenstance, or just plain dumb luck led the seasoned forerunners to it. I, for instance, had an unusual and totally unexpected career path leading to my focus on culture's influence on thought and behavior.

3.1 Montana Roots

As an undergraduate at the University of Montana in the mid-1950s I was a motivated student who earned mediocre grades.

I came from a blue-collar extended family in which no member had ever graduated from college. I was a good sprinter and my legs paid my way through four years of college. I took a broad assortment of classes but had only two courses in psychology, both elective. One was the introductory course, which I enjoyed because of the kindness of the instructor, and the other was a course in developmental psychology, which I did not enjoy because of the pompous arrogance of the instructor. I do not recall hearing the word "culture" in either of those classes or reading about culture in the required texts. But I fondly remember a course on world religions and was impressed with both the instructor and the multiplicity of religions on the planet. Honestly, I just didn't have the maturity and the dedicated scholarship it takes to understand the power that culture has in shaping lives. But growing up in the rough-and-tumble copper mining city of Butte, Montana probably helped me appreciate the panorama of human diversity. Butte provided a kaleidoscope of cultures and languages. Among my network of neighborhood friends were boys (mainly) and girls whose parents immigrated from Yugoslavia, Greece, England, Ireland, Austria, Germany, and Finland, along with an exchange student from Korea. My maternal and paternal grandparents had English and Swedish roots, respectively.

The early trajectory of my occupational life pointed to the US Air Force, and possibly a 20- or 30-year military career. That adventure ended in disappointment and, sometimes, despair and utter self-assessment. So, after three years of required active duty and reaching the rank of captain, I returned to my alma mater to continue my education that, I hoped, would lead to a satisfying career in some professional capacity. In 1960, and a few years older than most graduate students, I was offered a part-time job as a psychometrist in the student counseling center. Woefully unprepared for rigorous academic work at the graduate school level, I was surprised when asked to be a research assistant for two popular instructors in the small department of psychology. They must have liked the residue of military habits and the earnestness for further education that

I displayed. Thus began five years of continuous academic instruction, largely on a part-time basis because of the necessity of simultaneous blue-collar employment (primarily in the lumber mills) to help pay the bills.

An incident in a seminar in learning theory was important in helping to turn my attention to culture. The instructor, a fine teacher and prominent researcher, often described in detail his experiments. After class one day, I went to his office and in essence sheepishly asked him this question (as I remember it): "The highly verbal tasks you ask your subjects to perform assume that they are equally familiar with the English language and at times its various quaint idioms. Aren't the things you ask them to do unfair to, for example, subjects whose first or preferred language is something other than English?" He replied by telling me that if any volunteer subject was not a native speaker of English, he or she would be summarily dismissed from the experiment because he wanted to avoid dealing with "error variance." I didn't argue the point but immediately thought, "How strange it is to systematically eliminate participants from experiments, the results of which, when published, would putatively extend to all humans. Why not include all sorts of people in such experiments and take their responses into consideration when analyzing the data? Why purify or sanitize the subject pool?"[1]

3.2   Kurt Lewin's Influence on My Nascent Interest in Culture's Role

At the University of Montana the topological psychology of Kurt Lewin (1936) grabbed my attention. His ideas were a refreshing relief from the mechanistic theories of B. F. Skinner, Clark Hull, Kenneth Spence, Edward Tolman, John B. Watson, and others.

---

[1] A colleague, J. W. Berry, told a similar story. Years ago he asked one of his colleagues, who often used undergraduates to study social behavior, what he did in his classes that were becoming increasingly culturally diverse. His answer: "To me, culture is just noise." Berry's response: "To me, culture is music" (Berry, 2013, p. 56).

I was introduced to Lewin's unorthodox theory in a series of courses on personality and learning theory. Lewin, who was often identified with the Gestalt school of thought and then became a central figure in developing social psychology, leadership, and organizational dynamics, coined many new terms and added self-drawn sketches to help explain his central point: that behavior is the joint function of a specific and unique person operating in the "life space" (essentially culture) presented to him or her, all the time, by specific and unique environments that can only be interpreted by that person in that context. I imagined that the behavior of anyone could be explained by how he or she navigated in Lewin's world of vectors, valences, psychological barriers, etc. that differed among people. I even did a study that required samples of students to draw maps of their daily meanderings around the attractive campus and asked them to explain what they typically saw while doing so. In my view, everyone interpreted his or her world in highly personal ways and never duplicated what others saw, heard, or thought, even though they all lived in the same objective environment.

Instead of conforming to Aristotelian (linear, orthodox) thinking, which assumes needs, motives, and the like residing *within* the person, Lewin favored Galilean (nonlinear, unorthodox) thinking. To him, causation resides *outside* the person, and is primarily influenced by dynamic psychological facts of which the person is aware at any given moment. His principle of contemporaneity states that only those present facts influence thinking and behavior. One can readily understand, then, why the life space of an Australian aborigine in his or her vast desert would trigger different thought processes than those of an urban dweller in Jakarta, Indonesia, whose life space was enclosed within an extremely dense population and a complex array of stimuli. These differences in life experiences are major reasons why many culture-oriented psychologists tend to avoid using dependent and independent variables in their research. The intense study of behavior in context is the forte of cultural psychologists (see, for example, Boesch, 1991; Cole, 1996;

Valsiner, 2007, 2009). The *meaningfulness* of stimuli in one's life space is extraordinarily important.

Lewin's equation – B = f(P + E) (Behavior is a function of the Person and his or her Environment) – is elemental, especially when one considers that it is the person's *subjective* interpretation of a unique environment that creates the action. By current nomenclature Lewin would be called a cultural psychologist. He is still regarded as one of the giants in social psychology and was often described as "the complete social scientist" (Gold, 1999). One could argue that Lewin was one of the pioneers in the kind of theorizing espoused by culture-oriented psychologists, despite the fact that he never mentioned "culture" in the rather small seminal 1936 book that laid out his theory. He did, however, mention static "physical worlds" and dynamic "psychological worlds." One of the foundational figures in cross-cultural psychology, Harry Triandis, made similar points that included his well-known distinction between objective culture and subjective culture (Triandis, 1972). I also see many similarities between Lewin and the late cultural psychologist Ernest Boesch and his Symbolic Action Theory (Boesch, 1991; Lonner & Hayes, 2007). I come back to Boesch later in this Element.

3.3   Next Steps in a Forest of Indecision: Minnesota –
A New Awakening

Nearing the end of graduate school at Montana, I gave serious thought to applying for a job in the Nome, Alaska school system, primarily because working with Native Alaska children and their families sounded attractive and challenging. Instead, I spent a - final year at Montana as the assistant dean of students with the title of dean of men. My rather quixotic ventures next found me working for a year as school psychologist and track coach in a small Montana high school.

Yearning for more education and larger vistas, I next entered a PhD program at the University of Minnesota. It was there, in late 1963, at that bastion of Jeffersonian democracy and one of the institutions known as the "dustbowl of empiricism," that I became thoroughly smitten by the largely ignored concept of culture in psychology. In a required class titled "differential psychology" (individual differences), the instructor, John Darley, then chair of the psychology department, gave the class of about 20 graduate students some sage advice on the first day. He advised us to write the initials *IOC* in the margins of all pages in the required edited text containing many chapters on individual differences in various psychological subdomains. Explaining that the letters *IOC* are the initials for **I**n **O**ur **C**ulture, he emphasized that, while each chapter contained information that may well be valid for and in the United States, it may not be valid in other parts of the world.

In retrospect, I believe it was that incident, primed by my Montana experiences, that sold me completely on the proposition that all human thought and behavior can be, and should be, understood in specific cultural contexts. This was not an epochal idea, of course, but it seemed to be woefully understudied in contemporary psychology. Thus, early in 1964 I knew that I would dedicate my career to the psychological study of culture. I had no specific plan of action to do so, but I knew then that I could never again look at all of psychology's major and often brilliant corpus of theories and research without carefully considering the culture from which the theory and research came. In short, I became a cross-cultural psychologist. (But I did not yet have the gravitas, experience, or knowledge to identify myself as such. That was to come later.)

As I have described in somewhat greater detail elsewhere (Lonner, 2015), a series of events – some planned and others happenstance, circumstance, and old-fashioned good luck – led to what was to become a career-enhancing involvement with cross-cultural psychology. In effect, I had the good fortune to get involved with initiatives that culminated in the formal institutionalizing of cross-cultural psychology. Before I describe that, however, a short review of some background information about the role played by culture in psychology may be helpful.

3.4 When Did the Study of the "Other" Start? Ancients, Ancestors, Precursors, and Pioneers

Leaving personal influences for a moment, let's consider some historical information. As many scholars have noted, no one seems to know exactly when the term "culture" was first used to help explain the nature of groups of people who clustered together as cohesive units. Equally unknown is when the terms "cross-cultural" or "cross-cultural psychology" appeared in discussions about how people in various groups talked or thought about themselves and others. Excellent reviews on this topic are available (Klineberg, 1980; Jahoda, 1982; Jahoda & Krewer, 1997), and it is included in any good course of study on human origins. Klineberg began his chapter with the following deft paragraph:

> The interest in the behavior of "others," in the manner and morals of people different from (or similar to) one's own, undoubtedly began with the first contacts across national or tribal boundaries. It is unlikely that such contacts led to true understanding; since in so many languages the expression "the people" referred only to one's own group, it is not surprising that other groups were usually considered strange, exotic, inferior, and somewhat less than human. Even at a more sophisticated level, Herodotus, who lived in the fifth century, B. C., wrote of the "barbarians" who spoke no Greek, and whom he contrasted, to their disadvantage, with those fortunate to live in the (democratic) Greek city states. Although he travelled widely in the regions of the Eastern Mediterranean, and wrote interestingly and wisely of the habits and beliefs which he encountered, this "father of history" did not hide his satisfaction at the evident superiority of his own people. The belief that difference could be equated with inferiority has had a wide, if not universal distribution. The Chinese Emperor Ch'ien Lung wrote to George III of England in 1793: We possess all things, I set no value on objects

strange or ingenious, and have no use for your country's manufactures.

Herodotus's ethnocentric observations may be among the first ever reported by scholars. But as Klineberg noted, many additional scholars in antiquity could be mentioned. Miroglio, in his book *La psychologie des peoples*, referred to Herder in Germany, Vico in Italy, and Frazer in England, among others. Beginning in 1860 Lazarus and Steinthal edited the *Zeitschrift fur Volkerpsychologie und Sprachwissenschaft* for 30 years. Their scope was wide and included what could be called social psychology, the psychology of culture, and the "concrete psychology of people" from a comparative and especially a linguistic perspective.

Some years after Klineberg's observations were penned, Cole (1996) offered similar observations about the forerunners of the study of culture, and so did Jahoda (1992, 2011) and others. And, of course, there was Wilhelm Wundt, the so-called father of experimental psychology, whose contributions were immense. Over a 14-year period (1900–1914) Wundt published a series of volumes in his *Völkerpsychologie*, which is usually translated as *Indigenous Psychology* (Wundt, 1900–1920). Students of culture are also familiar with the name of W. H. R. Rivers and his Cambridge University expeditions many years ago (Rivers, 1901). Any contemporary and thorough text dealing with psychology and culture will have an extensive overview of these historical perspectives.

4 Aspects of the Current Scene: The Modern Era of Culture and Psychology

I and my fellow veterans in cross-cultural and cultural psychology have often been asked when the modern interest in the role of culture in psychology began. A definitive answer to this question usually begins with, "it depends on what you mean by 'modern' and also whom you ask." A timeline can vary a great deal and so can its interpretation. But in my opinion, the mid- to late 1960s was the period when the table was set for many activities that tended to define future steps. For me personally, 1965 was a key year. I had finished my two and a half years of graduate work at the University of Minnesota and began searching for a dissertation topic that I knew would be completed somewhere other than the United States. As I had been telling many friends and colleagues, it was time to go abroad, see some of the rest of the world, and do something meaningful. I yearned to do something of value, of character, of purpose.

4.1   A Stroke of Good Fortune

With enough funds to sustain myself at life-support level for a few months, I left for Sweden in November 1965, fully expecting to spend a year or two in the country that my paternal grandparents had left about 1900. I had even prepared myself for more effective communication by learning an acceptable level of Swedish while at the University of Minnesota – an effort that also satisfied the University of Minnesota's requirement that its doctoral candidates have a reading knowledge of at least two languages other than English (my other was German). While in Sweden I earned some pocket money by translating Swedish psychology manuscripts into English for international distribution. With a few permanent job prospects drying up, I left Sweden early in 1966, hitching a ride with a small family from Canada that was touring Europe in a Volkswagen bus. They dropped me off in Frankfurt, where, so I had heard, job prospects might be better for a wayfaring academic in search of a professional identity. In Frankfurt I applied for two jobs – one as a lecturer for the University of Maryland's European division, and the other as a school psychologist in Frankfurt Elementary School No. 2, which was part of the US military educational system for dependent children. After an adventurous, cathartic regenerating trip to Israel via the Orient Express, in mid-January 1966 I returned to Frankfurt and learned that I got both jobs. This was truly a remarkable turn of events, wonderfully capped by meeting Marilyn Sika from rural Oregon who was a second-grade teacher in the aforementioned school. I proposed to her on February 2 and we were married in Basel, Switzerland on April 26. Now, nearly 52 years later, we are still happily married and our three children produced a total of six grandchildren, all healthy and happy girls with bright futures.

On the quest for a dissertation that initially fueled my desire to go abroad, it might have been more challenging, and certainly more romantic, had I found some exotic topic in deep sub-Saharan Africa or some remote village in Mongolia. However, with a new wife and a desire to start, finally, a fulfilling career, I chose a topic that satisfied my thirst to add a different dimension to the literature on measuring interests, values, and attitudes. Under the guidance, by mail, of my dissertation advisor at Minnesota, I translated the Strong Vocational Interest Blank (SVIB) into German and measured the interests of German, Swiss, and Austrian psychologists and accountants. This was the first time that the popular SVIB had been translated and used in a language other than English, and in countries other than the United States. Unbeknownst to me at the time, it was similar to what German researchers had done with the famous Minnesota Multiphasic Personality Inventory (MMPI) a few years earlier (Spreen & Spreen, 1963). Both projects were largely detailed efforts to translate many brief items that were usually closely tied to idiomatic American English and therefore were exercises in trying to establish translation equivalence – a methodological procedure that is almost always a critical part of culture-comparative research involving questionnaires, directions, rankings, and other psychological measurement procedures (see later in this volume).

A manuscript reporting the main results of my dissertation was published roughly two years later in the *American Psychologist* (Lonner, 1968). That it appeared in the same issue as an article by Martin Luther King Jr. was an appreciated and welcome coincidence because of the immense role King had played in the tumultuous 1960s and the civil rights movement. There was also a certain irony in the dissertation process. Extending the SVIB to Europe was, as already noted, largely a translation project, but posed a key question: Will it work outside a country where the responses and norms had been fully developed since 1927, when

E. K. Strong introduced his method of measuring interests? Or was, and is, the SVIB simply an "emic" device that cannot be transferred, as an "imposed etic," to other cultural or linguistic populations? This is an enduring question in nearly all culture-comparative research involving the measurement of any manner of devices designed to put a number on human functioning. Adding a romantic interlude to the project, these and other issues in culture-comparative research were featured at a small conference held in the castle used in filming the famous movie *The Sound of Music*, with beautiful Salzburg, Austria as the setting.

An article by Wesley and Karr (1966) that focused on these questions was one of the scarce relevant methodological references available in the 1960s. I used it for guidance. The article appeared in the *International Journal of Psychology* (IJP), a new journal inaugurated in 1966, sponsored by the International Union of Psychological Science and featuring culture-oriented research reports. Just a short time later, and with no inkling it would happen, I played the main role in founding the JCCP, which soon became the IJP's main "competitor" (see later in this volume).

The disappointments and uncertainties of the previous five years in my checkered career were radically abating. With growing certainty that an academic career would be satisfying, my wife and I returned to the United States in 1967 and I received my PhD in December of that year. Our first stop was Oregon, my wife's home state where she grew up on a farm. Availing myself of an unusual opportunity, I accepted a position in the science education department at Oregon State University, in Corvallis. My main job, aided by a National Science Foundation grant, was to teach the rudimentary elements of Piagetian theory to a small group of visiting faculty members from several universities in India. This was my first position as an academic, and I enjoyed it. The first of our three children, a boy, was born in Corvallis in 1968, giving further proof that things were strongly coalescing in my favor.

By sheer happenstance, opportunity came knocking in March 1968 when I applied and was interviewed for an opening as an assistant professor in the department of psychology (and part time in the student counseling center) at Western Washington State College (Western Washington University since 1977, and hereafter called Western). During the job interview I told the late Merle E. Meyer, then department chair, that if I was hired I wanted to devote my career to the interface between the discipline of psychology and the phenomenon of culture. I was hired, and Meyer acceded to my wishes and became my main supporter on campus. Thus, on September 1, 1968, I was finally on a definite career path, but it was not yet clear where that path would take me. I was eager to find out.

4.2 Entering the World of Cross-Cultural Psychology: Helping to Shape the Early Years

My new position abruptly ushered me into a small but rapidly growing nucleus of culture-oriented psychologists and other scholars throughout the world. I knew none of them personally, but had heard of some. Many were already accomplished scholars who not only shared my interest in the connections between culture and psychology but had already done research in the area. Robert D. Meade had joined the department at Western two years earlier. He also viewed culture as an essential component in all things psychological. Although he was not present during my earlier visit to Western, I quickly learned that several months earlier Bob, who died in 2015, had attended a conference at the East-West Center in Hawaii titled "Psychological Problems in Changing Societies."

4.3 The 1966 East-West Center Conference

Funded by the US Office of Naval Research and organized and chaired by F. Kenneth Berrien of Rutgers University, the conference was attended by approximately 22 psychologists from the United States and Pacific Rim countries (one woman – Edith D. Neimark, a developmental psychologist also of Rutgers, participated in the conference). It focused largely on what today would be called acculturation and adaptation issues in a growing world.

Berrien had a strong interest in the ethics of cross-cultural research (Berrien, 1966). Unfortunately, he died in 1971 at the young age of 63, and a much-belated tribute is warranted. I never met him, but there is little doubt that he would have been a major influence in shaping the development of cross-cultural psychology. He attended the earlier Ibadan conference (see Section 4.4), and his involvement there led to the East-West Center conference. Ken was a frequent contributor to the increasing activities in cross-cultural psychology. He published several articles in the young *International Journal of Psychology* (IJP). One focused on Japanese and American values (Berrien, 1966), a second concerned methodological and related problems in cross-cultural research (Berrien, 1967), and a third dealt with stereotyping and social desirability between Japanese and Americans (Berrien, 1969). The year before his death he wrote about the ethics of cross-cultural research, a piece in which he called for a "super-ego for cross-cultural research" (Berrien, 1970). In that unprecedented article he noted that "one of the chief instruments contributing to the expansion of cross-cultural studies has been the jet airplane. Relatively inexpensive in money and amazingly inexpensive in time, it has permitted more researchers to rub together in ways, and with a frequency never before possible" (p. 33). Thus, "jet-set" research and sabbatical opportunism increased. Accompanying that advance were increases in the chances of creating certain ethical problems.

To help counter this rise in ethical problems, Berrien (1970) wrote that the best cross-cultural research

1) Engages the efforts of two or more investigators of different countries,
2) Has strong support from institutions in all countries involved in the research,
3) Addresses researchable problems of concern to both countries,
4) Focuses on relevant social problems,
5) Encourages the joint definition of the problems,

6) Uses comparable methods,
7) Pools data that would be jointly owned by the countries involved,
8) Reports researchers' own interpretations to their own constituents, but
9) Is obliged to strive for interpretations acceptable to a world community of scholars.

More than a decade later, Warwick (1980) wrote about the politics and ethics of cross-cultural research, but curiously did not cite Berrien. Nevertheless, his influence in the early days was profound. He accepted my invitation to be a consulting editor for the JCCP. One can only imagine the nature of his contributions had he lived another decade or two.

The East-West Center group followed through with a newsletter that lasted a few years. It was designed to communicate reports of activities, plans, research results, and so forth among those who attended the conference. The May 1969 issue announced that

> Under the editorship of Walter J. Lonner, Western Washington State College, Bellingham, Washington, the *Journal of Cross-Cultural Studies* [*sic*] is being launched this year. This will provide an additional and specialized outlet for research of the kind in which we are interested. Heretofore the *Journal of Social Psychology* and the *International Journal of Psychology* had been receptive to cross-cultural reports but have included a much wider range of articles.

4.4   The 1966–1967 Ibadan Conference

I also quickly learned that a year and a half earlier a similar conference was held from late December 1966 to early January 1967 at the University of Ibadan, Nigeria. Organized by Herbert Kelman (who at age 91 still teaches at Harvard) and Henri Tajfel (who died in 1982 at age 62), the conference, attended by about 50 scholars, had as its purpose to bring psychologists and other social scientists from Africa and the West together, in the hope that they could develop research collaborations. Similar in scope to the 1966 East-

West Center's workshop mentioned earlier, that conference was successful in bringing primarily social psychologists together to discuss social psychological problems in developing countries. The most important offshoot of the Ibadan conference was the inauguration of the *Cross-Cultural Social Psychology Newsletter*. The *Newsletter*, the first issue of which was dated March 1967, was to include letters, abstracts, and news items relevant to the themes of the conference. Harry Triandis edited the *Newsletter* during its first year, and Yasumasa Tanaka followed him for a few years. This mimeographed and uncopyrighted publication reached a fair number of psychologists. When the IACCP was inaugurated in 1972, the *Newsletter* became part of that effort. It gradually morphed into the *Cross-Cultural Psychology Bulletin*, with William K. Gabrenya Jr. serving as editor for many years. The *Bulletin* continues to be an important activity of the IACCP. For more details and informative perspectives about the early years of this activity, see IACCP.org.

These two conferences, half a world apart and in reasonably close temporal proximity, were, in retrospect, evidence that mainstream psychology, with its narrowness and hegemonic parochialism – albeit benign, with no sinister intentions – no longer fit the modern and rapidly changing world. Despite ample and obvious evidence that there were many culture-oriented psychologists throughout the world in the 1960s, and certain universities that were enlightened in that direction, I have heard of no other conferences that were attended by psychologists from many countries and cultures that appeared during that decade. This paucity of gatherings of like-minded psychologists was soon to change in many ways.

4.5   The Center for Cross-Cultural Research

Largely in response to the tenor of the times and a conjunction of events, in January 1969 the Center for Cross-Cultural Research at Western was established. Endorsed in principle by the college president, appropriate deans, and the department of psychology, the basic structure was laid out. Meade, my senior in age, rank, and experience, was appointed as its director and I as associate director. I also enthusiastically seized the opportunity to launch what was soon to become the *Journal of Cross-Cultural Psychology* (JCCP). It was agreed by all that if such a journal was to become a reality, I would become its founding editor.

Several other members of the department of psychology became associates of the Center. Also, the dean of the Bureau for Faculty Research, an anthropologist who received his doctorate from the University of Chicago, granted my request of $1,000 to cover the initial expenses needed to put it all together. He did this with some reluctance, and offered the slightly deflating opinion that the effort would likely fail anyway, thereby absolving him of responsibility for any additional financial support. I told him that I wouldn't let it fail. As I explain in more detail in what follows, the JCCP enriched Western – both academically and financially – far more than anyone expected. Unfortunately, Taylor did not live long enough to see how his small but necessary grant led to such gains. It would have been fun to return his $1,000, with interest and a friendly and thankful, wry smile.

4.6   The Journals

The establishment of the JCCP was a significant development that required some cautious thought before going forward with the idea. An assessment of the professional psychology journals, worldwide, in the late 1960s resulted in my identifying about 50 that would occasionally, and a few of them often, publish articles of the type we envisioned. We also discovered that no extant psychology journal in the world had the words "culture" or "cross-cultural" as part of its title.

Continuing with caution, between October 1968 and March 1969 we conducted a worldwide survey of behavioral scientists to help us determine the need for a journal exclusively devoted to cross-cultural psychological research. We devised a simple survey describing our proposal to inaugurate a quarterly peer-reviewed international interdisciplinary journal that would be exclusively cross-cultural. The survey contained four key questions: 1) Do you think such a journal is needed? 2) Would you submit manuscripts to it? 3) Would you subscribe to it? and 4) Would you encourage your institutional library to subscribe to it? We also requested from publishers in many countries complimentary copies of psychology and anthropology journals so that we could examine their content and masthead policies. We received dozens of them and examined them carefully. Two major findings resulting from these efforts were that about 97% of the 250 (of 350) who responded to the survey were enthusiastic about inaugurating such a journal, and that about 50 journals published cross-cultural articles, in greatly varying numbers.

Our main concern was the possibility that the JCCP might encroach on the territory covered by existing journals. For instance, the *Journal of Social Psychology*, an APA publication, already featured a section titled "Cross-Cultural Notes." Its editor, Leonard W. Doob, nevertheless became one of my strongest supporters, and in a sense a mentor by mail during the start-up period. The matter that concerned me most was the quarterly IJP. Launched in 1966, endorsed by the United Nations Educational, Social, and Cultural Organization (UNESCO), and funded in its early years by the Aquinas Fund, it became the official journal of the International Union of Psychological Science (IUPsyS), which was established in 1950. Germaine de Montmollin of Paris, a social psychologist, was its first editor. In its first year of publication, 42 of 76 articles were decidedly cross-cultural, and more than half of the authors were from the United States. Concerned that so much space was being given to cross-cultural articles, but pleased that the journal was doing its intended job, the IUPsyS proposed that it should mainly address "fundamental theoretical issues" in psychology that might apply everywhere. The International Platform section of the IJP was also appraised, and its continuation was assured. The quarterly received 400 subscriptions the first year, a somewhat lower figure than expected, given that it was the only journal published by the largest psychological association in the world, and the second oldest (the International Association of Applied Psychology was formed in 1919).

Examining the world of psychology journals at that time (perhaps more than 600 of them in many countries and languages), we were nearly certain that the JCCP would be unique in publishing only articles that exclusively involved the interaction between psychological phenomena and culture. Thus, the JCCP was to become the first refereed periodical in psychology that included either "culture" or "cross-cultural" in its title. Incidentally, Germaine de Montmollin, in her role as the IJP's inaugural editor, wrote me in late 1969 and pointedly asked if I thought it wise or necessary to go ahead with our plans to produce a journal that she thought would duplicate their efforts. In my diplomatic response I mildly argued that I and many others did not think it would mimic their efforts. I of course thanked her for her interest. Unfortunately, I did not keep that correspondence. I was pleased and continued to be relieved that the JCCP did not encroach on or dampen their efforts, for the IJP continues to play an important part in international psychology.

In the process of learning as much as I could about the nature, stature, and scope of cross-cultural research in the 1960s, I noticed frequent references to the Human Relations Area Files (HRAF). The brainchild of anthropologist George Peter Murdock, the HRAF, located at Yale University and inaugurated in 1937, had become a popular tool in comparative anthropological research. It is incumbent upon neophytes in this area of research to learn the details of the HRAF. With its clever alphanumeric system of outlining cultural materials and world cultures, familiarity with the HRAF is a must (see HRAF.org).

I spent the better part of 1969 doing the many things necessary to put together a journal that would have all the components required of a professional periodical. The most important structural component was creating a clear masthead policy and putting together an editorial advisory board. Devoid of any experience with the workings of any journal and almost no professional acquaintances who might have guided me, I forged ahead. Because I wanted the new journal to have broad academic appeal, the subtitle was "International and Interdisciplinary." Guided by their influences in the literature and name recognition, members of the initial editorial advisory board included three associate editors (Harrison Gough of the University of California at Berkeley, Daniel Katz of the University of Michigan – both influential psychologists in different subfields of the discipline, and Yasumasa Tanaka, a political scientist and psychologist from Gakushuin University in Tokyo. Thirty-six scholars from 20 countries and several academic disciplines comprised the list of consulting editors. The willingness of such scholars as David McClelland, of need for achievement fame; Leonard W. Doob, the very experienced editor of the *Journal of Social Psychology*; the well-known Henri Tajfel of England; F. Kenneth Berrien; and other accomplished behavioral scientists to serve as consultants was humbling. I was gratified that so many scholars responded enthusiastically, especially because I was virtually unknown and much less experienced in the field. Most of them have died, and I am the only person who remains from the original editorial board, currently carrying the title of founding and special issues editor. My dedication to the JCCP and to cross-cultural psychology generally is, next to my family, my greatest source of pride because it became the flagship journal in the field and a signal entity in the ascent of cross-cultural psychology.

An important part of the plan was to produce a not-for-profit journal. The rationale for austerity was to produce a quarterly journal that might be affordable throughout the world, including the poorest countries. The initial one-year subscription rates of $7 for individuals and $10 for institutions, and even lower per annum rates for three-year subscriptions, were bargains. These rates would not have been possible if Western had not covered postal costs, or if I or anyone else had demanded compensation for their work. Subscription rates for 2017, set of course by Sage Publications, were $191 for individuals and $1,648 for institutions. However, the current costs are for an established journal that has grown from a quarterly to 10 issues per volume (year) and publishes far more articles. Still, without the low initial rates the JCCP may not have attracted as many initial subscriptions as it did.

Producing the JCCP at Western, decades before the Internet and other technical aids, became a small cottage industry. I was in charge of every facet of the operation: advertising, editing, subscriptions, banking, coordinating printing, and supervising occasional student help. Those tasks, as well as teaching full time and fulfilling family responsibilities, were rather overwhelming at times, but also constantly exciting because I enjoyed the challenge and knew that the venture would be successful.

With occasional concerns that there would not be enough accepted manuscripts to guarantee a smooth operational flow, the first year was satisfying and promising. The number of subscriptions, even at the bargain rates we offered, brought in enough money, and increased my confidence that we could fund the operation on an intentional not-for-profit basis. We had little overhead, were graced by the availability of an expert typist in Western's Bureau for Faculty Research, used the archaic photo-offset method for printing, and qualified for reduced postal rates. The submission of manuscripts picked up to such an extent that our rejection rate reached 80%, thus giving us confidence that we would have a sufficient base of accepted manuscripts for continued routine publication. Articles by the late Gustav Jahoda and John Berry, two scholars in the area, appeared the first year.

It turned out that an article by Richard W. Brislin, titled "Back-Translation for Cross-Cultural Research" (Brislin, 1970), was the star of the first year of publication. It is still referenced, and in terms of citations, probably ranks among the top 25 journal articles in the now-mammoth cross-cultural literature. Moreover, Brislin joined the Center in 1972, but lasted only two years before leaving for the East-West Center's Culture Learning Institute. Not long after Brislin left, Merle Meyer, who was so kindly supportive, accepted an offer to become chair of the department of psychology at the University of Florida. He wanted to take me with him, but I am a denizen of the Pacific Northwest, with its rain, mountains, fir trees, and wildlife.

In the JCCP's inaugural year I was buoyed by a brief article written by Jahoda, an early leader in the psychological study of culture and the first full-term president of the IACCP. Shortly after the first issue of the JCCP was published he sent me a congratulatory letter and an offprint of an article he had recently published. I cherish what he wrote; he noted, in part, that psychology's constrained borders reminded him of

> Parson Thwackum in Tom Jones [Henry Fielding's humorous 1749 novel about a commoner being raised among the English nobility], who said, "When I mention religion, I mean the Christian religion, and not only the Christian religion, but the Protestant religion, and not only [the] Protestant religion, but the Church of England." This might well be suitably transposed as "When I mention a psychological subject, I mean a subject from a Western industrialized culture, and not only a Western industrialized culture, but an American, and not only an American but a college student." No doubt this is unfair, reflecting as it does the amount of work that has been done in the United States. Nonetheless, the excessive concentration on such an odd (as far as humanity at large is concerned) population makes one wonder about the range of "laws" experimentally derived in this manner.   (Jahoda, 1970, p. 2)

I have often referred to that Dickensian phrasing because, to me, it captured the essence of why I devoted so much time to the development of the JCCP and why so many others wanted to break out of the restricted cultural box in which contemporary psychology found itself.

So, the future was looking bright for the Center and especially for the JCCP. Things were excellent on the home front as well, for on January 10, 1971, we had our third and last child, Andrea. Quite literally, I watched our children and the JCCP grow up together. I fondly refer to the JCCP as "my baby." Ironically, our second child, Alyssa, is currently chair of the department of German and Russian at Wake Forest University. That department is in the same building, Green Hall, as the department of psychology, and the

JCCP's current editor, Deborah L. Best, has an office right above our daughter's office. Small world.

5   A Sea Change in the Development of Cross-Cultural Psychology

The immediate success of the JCCP and the growing confidence that we happened to be at the right place at the right time drew attention on two fronts. First, and historically the most important to hundreds of dedicated culture-oriented psychologists, was the foresight shown and explained by John L. M. Dawson. Dawson, an Australian psychologist with research experience in Africa, had recently moved to Hong Kong to head the department of psychology at the University of Hong Kong. Prior to his move, he and John Berry had discussions about creating some kind of mechanism or association that would bring together psychologists from many countries who were interested in exploring connections between psychology and culture. Dawson got to work.

Dawson wrote to me in mid-1971, inquiring about a possible union of our respective endeavors. Explaining that he was planning to organize and chair a conference at his university the following year, he suggested a merger. The conference would attract, he estimated, more than 100 psychologists from many countries who had demonstrated a strong interest in cross-cultural psychology. The three-day gathering was to inaugurate the IACCP. Dawson wondered if I would be interested in looking into the prospect of the JCCP becoming the official journal of the IACCP. Realizing that there is strength in numbers and intuiting that professional journals tended to thrive better if they had a professional home, I valued this inquiry and did what was necessary to complete an agreement that would be mutually advantageous. The agreement, endorsed by Western, the copyright holder, was that Western would continue ownership of the JCCP, but the IACCP would be allowed to call the JCCP its official publication. That seemed to me a workable trade-off, especially because if the JCCP had not already existed, the association may well have inaugurated its own journal, thereby making its mark and creating a stream of income. Had the JCCP not existed at the time, I have often wondered if the soon-to-be-inaugurated IACCP would have started its own journal. My guess is that it would not have, because several of the more experienced psychologists at the inaugural meeting had previously expressed their satisfaction with the IJP and other journals, such as the popular *Journal of Personality and Social Psychology*. Similarly, I have wondered if the JCCP would have survived without being attached to some larger group. In either scenario, we will never know what would have happened.

The conference was a big success and was immediately preceded by the quadrennial IUPsyS conference, held in Tokyo. This was the first time that the IUPsyS met in Asia; the previous conferences were mainly in major European countries (exceptions being New Haven, Connecticut; Washington, DC; and Montreal). Many who attended the inaugural IACCP conference, including myself, attended the Tokyo conference. There were 110 participants in the Hong Kong inauguration. Many of them knew of each other via publications, but with a few exceptions had never met face to face. Everyone returned to their respective homes brimming with confidence that this marriage of factions would last. Roughly two years later a book containing selected readings from the presentations was published, becoming the first of many books containing the proceedings of biennial IACCP conferences (Dawson & Lonner, 1974).

5.1 The International Association for Cross-Cultural Psychology

Despite not yet topping 1,000 paid members, the IACCP was, and remains, the largest organization in the world that *exclusively* focuses on research and other scholarly activities involving the admixture of psychology and culture. It sponsors both international (even years) and regional (odd years) conferences, with the former scheduled in close proximity to either the much larger IUPsyS or the International Association of Applied Psychology

(IAAP) conferences, both of which meet quadrennially. The IACCP has all the trappings of a responsible and active international body of researchers and scholars, including a detailed constitution that is periodically updated and approved by the members.

Among the range of activities of the IACCP in the promotion of cross-cultural psychology is recognition of those who have made significant contribution to the field, as well as students who have demonstrated great potential. The former is in the category of Honorary Fellows and the latter includes the "Harry C. and Pola Triandis Outstanding Dissertation Award." Following is an alphabetical listing of Honorary Fellows of the IACCP, with country of birth in parentheses.

John W. Berry (Canada)	Walter J. Lonner (USA)
Deborah L. Best (USA)	Ruth H. Munroe (USA)†
Michael H. Bond (Canada)	Charles E. Osgood (USA)†
Jerome Bruner (USA)†	Janak Pandey (India)
John L. M. Dawson (Australia)†	Ype Poortinga (The Netherlands)
James Georgas (Greece)	Marshall Segall (USA)
Rogelio Díaz-Guerrero (Mexico)†	Shalom Schwartz (Israel)
Geert Hofstede (The Netherlands)	Durganand Sinha (India)†
Heidi Keller (Germany)	Peter B. Smith (UK)
Gustav Jahoda (Scotland)†	Harry C. Triandis (USA)
Çiğdem Kağıtçıbaşı (Turkey)†	Herman A. Witkin (USA)†
Daphne M. Keats (Australia)	

Detailed further information is available at IACCP.org. For information about numerous organizations and associations that focus to varying extents on cross-cultural, cultural, and multicultural psychology, please see Lonner, Keith, and Matsumoto (in press) and commentaries later in this volume.

The IACCP recently added another way to honor individuals who have made unusually significant contributions to cross-cultural psychology. Called the Outstanding Contributions Award, nominees do not have to be IACCP members, thus making it possible to recognize cultural psychologists, indigenous psychologists, and psychological anthropologists.

5.2 Enter Sage Publications

The second significant development also began when the JCCP was in its second year (1971). Sara Miller McCune, cofounder of Sage Publications, located in Beverly Hills, California, in the late 1960s, inquired about the prospect of moving publication of the JCCP to that fledgling company. I met with Sara and two of her senior staff members (there were only four such people on the staff at that time). We reached an agreement, and starting with Volume 4, in 1973, Sage printed and distributed the JCCP. The copyright remained at Western and all the conceptual and editorial responsibilities remained under my control. However, because of its close ties with the IACCP, the association's Communications and Publications Committee, in close conjunction with the JCCP's editorial board, have played a major role in all aspects of the JCCP. Early on, the modest royalties that Sage paid covered certain expenses, including traveling to special conferences. The financial situation changed radically in 2004 (see later in this volume).

I say more about Sage throughout the remainder of this Element. However, it is important to capture the essence of the excitement that these two developments – the IACCP and Sage, with its bold offer to publish a new and yet-to-be thoroughly tested journal – brought to the growing culture-oriented efforts in psychology. This excitement was enhanced by other events and publications, some of which I summarized in an editorial for the March 1973 issue of the JCCP – the first issue published by Sage under the new agreement. For instance, I noted that at the 1971 annual meeting of the APA, the Division 8 (Personality and Social) program had a cross-national theme, and at the same meeting, the International Council of Psychologists sponsored a symposium on cross-cultural research. Several books of integrated cross-cultural readings and others concentrating on theory and method have appeared, and still more are in preparation.

5.3   *Across Disciplines and Cultures*

I also noted that another development was the formation of the
Society for Cross-Cultural Research (SCCR), a federation consist-
ing of psychologists, anthropologists, and sociologists. The SCCR
held its first meeting in Pittsburgh in February 1972. Also, at the
annual convention of the Japanese Social Psychology Association
in November of that year, there was a meeting of Japanese cross-
cultural researchers. Further important impetus was given by the
1972 Istanbul conference, "Cultural Factors in Mental Tests," the
main results of which eventuated in the much-heralded edited
book, *Mental Tests and Cultural Adaptation* (Cronbach & Drenth,
1972). Shortly after that, early in 1973, the East-West Center's
Culture Learning Institute sponsored a seminar, "The Interface
between Culture and Learning." Emanating from that excellent
event was the edited book *Cross-Cultural Perspectives on
Learning* (Brislin, Bochner, & Lonner, 1975). Harry C. Triandis,
who had become a leading contributor to the field, attended that
conference, and it was at that gathering that plans to produce a
multivolume *Handbook of Cross-Cultural Psychology* were
announced and discussed. Another attendee was Michael Cole,
an influential psychologist who identified mainly with cultural
psychology, which was cross-cultural psychology's sister discipline
(or closest rival). Cole gained solid footage through his collabora-
tion with two Russian culture-oriented psychologists, Alexander
Luria and Lev Vygotsky (see later in this volume).

This collection of events in a narrow slice of time was a harbinger
of exciting developments. Unbeknownst to me and everyone else,
numerous activities were soon to unfold. I witnessed much of that
activity and contributed to it, and was positioned to participate in
an explosion of activities that featured cross-cultural psychology
and a number of other scholarly efforts.

6   Capturing the Essence of Cross-Cultural Psychology

I asserted earlier that a general consensus holds that the modern
era of cross-cultural psychology has covered a bit more than a 50-

year span. The movement started to gain traction in the 1960s, received further strength through the coalition of the IACCP and the JCCP, and continues unabated to the present day. Assuming that readers (and future contributors) of forthcoming Elements in the Psychology and Culture series may find it helpful, I want to present an annotated chronology of events and various contributions to this ongoing movement. To provide a semblance of order to the ever-increasing outpouring of publications and events during the past half-century, the next section gives a synopsis in five decade-long chunks: 1970–1979, 1980–1989, 1990–1999, 2000–2009, and 2010 to the present. Anchoring these five parcels with aspects of the part I know best – the IACCP–JCCP nexus – I begin each with a commentary on the decade. Additionally, I include essential information about all 23 biennial international conferences of the IACCP. An overview of selected important collateral contributions, events, and innovations, all of which involve culture in some fashion or form is given.

6.1   1970–1979: Building Foundations

The 1970s witnessed the development of foundations whose frameworks and innovations, as noted earlier, began to emerge in the 1960s. But with the exception of some culture-related activities sponsored by the IUPsyS and the IAAP, few efforts implemented or suggested the institutionalization of efforts that explicitly placed culture and all its variations at the center of scholarly efforts. In other words, despite several scattered activities that promoted deeper consideration of culture's influence on virtually every possible psychological topic, no concerted efforts took place at the broad organizational level to build a solid base for such activities. That changed radically, in many ways, in the decade of 1970–1979.

Reflecting on all that has occurred in the past half-century, I argue that the decade of the 1970s – richly fueled by important activities in the 1960s – sowed more foundational seeds at the international level than any other decade of development in the courtship involving culture and psychology. Not to diminish other decades that followed, for all of them have contributed important developments, I contend that the 1970s were truly the halcyon years of invigorating progress in the field. Importantly, this was also a period when a growing network of culture-oriented psychologists got to know one another in person, primarily during conferences, rather than on paper in the form of books and journal articles. As a bonus, I fondly remember the 1970s as an exciting period of personal growth as an academic psychologist and as a husband and father.

6.1.1   IACCP and JCCP Activities

The 1970s were marked by the appearance of the JCCP and by the first four IACCP conferences:

1970: Inauguration of the JCCP. Volume 1, No. 1 published in March. Lonner as founding editor and Western Washington State College (Center for Cross-Cultural Research, Department of Psychology) as copyright holder. The first three years of quarterly publication, including typing, editing, distribution, etc. – a virtual cottage industry – was done in Bellingham, Washington. As I briefly explained earlier, its inauguration was accompanied by two versions of the *Directory of Cross-Cultural Research and Researchers*. The first directory, compiled by J. W. Berry and published in the *International Journal of Psychology* in 1968 (Volume 3, No. 2), included an alphanumeric system for identifying the names, addresses, and areas of interests of culture-oriented psychologists. The second edition, edited by Berry and Lonner in 1970, was included, gratis, with subscriptions to the JCCP. The third edition, published in 1973, was edited by Berry, Lonner, and Jules Leroux, who was then editor of the IJP.

1972: Inaugural IACCP conference at the University of Hong Kong. J. L. M. B. Dawson, Hong Kong, conference president. Inaugural IACCP president: Jerome Bruner, USA, who immediately acceded to Gustav Jahoda, Scotland, the first full-term president. Inaugural president's introduction to the conference: Gustav Jahoda, secretary general: Harry C. Triandis, USA. Conference proceedings: *Readings in Cross-Cultural Psychology*. J. L. M. B. Dawson & W. J. Lonner, Eds. (University of Hong Kong Press, 1974).

1974: Second IACCP conference. Queen's University, Kingston, Ontario, Canada. Conference president: John W. Berry, Canada, presidential address: Applying Cross-Cultural Research to the Third World. Gustav Jahoda, Scotland, president-elect: Harry C. Triandis, USA, secretary-general: J. L. M. Dawson, Hong Kong. Conference proceedings: *Applied Cross-Cultural Psychology*. J. W. Berry & W. J. Lonner, Eds. (Swets & Zeitlinger, 1975).

1976: Third IACCP conference. Tilburg University, The Netherlands. Conference president: Ype H. Poortinga, The Netherlands, presidential address: Impediments to the Progress of Cross-Cultural Psychology. Harry C. Triandis, USA, president-elect: M. O. A. Durojaiye, Nigeria, secretary-general: John W. Berry, Canada. Conference proceedings: *Basic Problems in Cross-Cultural Psychology*. Y. H. Poortinga, Ed. (Swets & Zeitlinger, 1977).

1978: Fourth IACCP conference, Munich, West Germany. Conference president: Lutz H. Eckensberger, West Germany, presidential address: The Need for International Cooperation in Cross-Cultural Psychology with Special Reference to Action Research in Africa. M. A. O. Durojaiye, Nigeria, president-elect: J. L. M. Dawson, Hong Kong, secretary-general: J. W. Berry. Conference proceedings: *Cross-Cultural Contributions to Psychology*. L. H. Eckensberger, W. J. Lonner, & Y. H. Poortinga, Eds. (Swets & Zeitlinger, 1979).

6.1.2 Other Noteworthy Activities of the 1970s

The decade of the 1970s was rich with influential books and journal articles, many of them "firsts." The items mentioned in this section qualify as seminal because they addressed various issues and presented innovations. There were, of course, many books and journal articles, and other items that could be mentioned. The following are solid examples of scholarly approaches during the decade that helped usher in an impressive proliferation of books in the decades to come.

6.1.3 *The Handbook of Cross-Cultural Psychology* (HCCP)

Although the HCCP was published and copyrighted in 1980, it was essentially a product that began in the early 1970s. The influence of the HCCP – nothing like it had been published before – cannot be overstated. Many consider it the signal event that established cross-cultural psychology as an important and formidable event in the development of psychology. The *Handbook*, as it is generally called, was the idea of Jack Peters, an acquisitions editor at Allyn and Bacon. During the APA's annual convention in 1972 in Hawaii, Peters asked Triandis if he would be interested in editing such a handbook. Not certain that such an effort was needed, Peters and Triandis wrote to a number of well-traveled cross-cultural psychologists, seeking their opinions. They were almost unanimous in thinking that a handbook would be useful. This strong show of support mirrored the support we had received three years earlier when we surveyed a large number of psychologists throughout the world about inaugurating the JCCP.

At the East-West Center's conference on "The Interface between Culture and Learning" in January 1973, Triandis also surveyed the international group of psychologists in attendance. Strong support of the idea to produce a handbook continued. In the summer of 1973 Triandis completed a tentative outline and, realizing that he could not handle the project by himself, made the decision to enlist the assistance of several associate editors.

The next large step in the process of producing the HCCP took place in Chicago in 1975, during a meeting of the Society for Cross-Cultural Research, which itself was founded in 1971, thus giving further testimony to the vibrancy of activities afoot in culture-oriented psychology. A symposium at that meeting featured eight scholars, including Triandis, who, along with the audience, presented their ideas about the shape of the *Handbook*. Then, in January 1976 another conference occurred at the East-West Center. It was exclusively devoted to a more detailed discussion of the contents of the *Handbook*. About two-thirds of the chapters were thoroughly discussed, with a group of postdoctoral students, mainly from Asian countries, assisting in the entire process.

Everyone involved with the project was committed to producing a handbook with authors from every continent. Although this proved impossible, authors from nine countries were assigned to author or coauthor each of the 51 chapters distributed across the six volumes. Additionally, Triandis appointed a board of 20 regional editors. These editors prepared abstracts of publications not generally available to North American and European libraries. The abstracts were then sent to selected chapter authors, thus increasing the chapter authors' and eventual readers' exposure to literature not widely available. Thirteen of the 20 regional editors supplied useful information. Further details of the process appear in the preface Triandis wrote; it appears in all six volumes of the *Handbook*.

Because it was officially published in 1980, additional comments on the contents and influence of the Handbook are in the next section that features developments in the first full decade of the IACCP – the decade of 1980–1989.

6.1.4 Society for Cross-Cultural Research (SCCR)

Founded in 1971, the SCCR is a multidisciplinary organization. Its members share a common devotion to the conduct of cross-cultural research and include professionals and students from the social science fields of psychology, anthropology, and sociology; and related fields including education, family studies, social work, human development, psychiatry, communications, ethnic studies, business, and others. As noted on its website, a distinguishing characteristic of the SCCR, compared with other academic organizations, is that it is fundamentally interdisciplinary and provides members the opportunity to network with scholars from a wide variety of approaches to cross-cultural and comparative research. Like the IACCP and other professional associations, the SCCR has hosted conferences that offer members and participants the opportunity to better know each other, form productive and lasting relationships, and provide genuine support to their fellow colleagues and students.

The SCCR journal, *Cross-Cultural Research*, publishes articles spread across many disciplines. The journal was originally titled *Behavior Science Notes* (in 1966), and then called *Behavior Science Research*. In the 1990s it expanded its focus and became a peer-reviewed journal. The SCCR is academically linked to the Human Relations Area Files, and its website contains links to many international resources (www.sccr.org). Clearly, it grew out of initiatives developed in the 1970s, but its roots go back to the late 1930s when anthropologist George Peter Murdock played the major role in creating the Human Relations Area Files.

6.1.5 The *International Journal of Intercultural Relations (IJIR)*

The IJIR appeared in 1977 as a quarterly, peer-reviewed journal. The main impetus for its founding was the realization that members of a number of disciplines were conducting culture-oriented research, and that these disciplines could benefit from an exchange of diverse points of view. Psychology, education, communications, anthropology, sociology, and marketing are among the academic orientations represented, thereby making the IJIR similar to *Cross-Cultural Research*. The IJIR is especially strong in publishing such topics as acculturation and immigration issues, as well as various problems and issues encountered by individuals coping with intercultural adjustment. I was pleased to be on the editorial board for a number of years. The IJIR, with founding editor Dan Landis then at the helm, is the main publication of the International Academy of Intercultural Research (IAIR), an interdisciplinary organization officially established in 1997. The current editor is Dina Birman. The IAIR holds biennial conferences in various parts of the world. Complete details appear at www.interculturalacadecy.org.

6.1.6 *Mind, Culture and Activity: An International Journal* (MAC)

The MAC is an upscale version of the *Quarterly Newsletter of the Laboratory of Comparative Human Cognition* (QNLCHC), which began in the late 1970s. The main person behind its founding was

Michael Cole, an accomplished cultural psychologist. The LCHC is a social sciences laboratory at the University of California at San Diego; its influences are many, including cultural anthropology, American pragmatism, and Soviet psychology. Of the latter, the ideas of Alexander Luria and Lev Vygotsky have been of special importance to Cole and his network of international scholars.

Like other culture-oriented perspectives in psychology, cultural psychology such as the type espoused by the LCHC, grew out of major human tragedies and movements, such as World War II and the founding of the United Nations, the Korean and Viet Nam conflicts, the US civil rights movement, and other unrests such as the People's Revolution in China. All of these events funneled into the 1960s, eventually giving rise to the wealth of activities of the very busy 1970s.

6.1.7 Introduction of Psychological Anthropology

For many years the subfield of culture and personality was an influential perspective in anthropology. Led by scholars such as anthropologist Clyde Kluckhohn and psychologist Henry Murray (of Thematic Apperception Test fame), it attracted many researchers. However, over the years this subfield fell out of favor and was replaced at the behest of one of the many anthropologists who championed a change. Thus, in the introduction to his edited text, *Psychological Anthropology*, which was heralded as a "new edition," Francis Hsu wrote, "with these thoughts on the central concerns of culture-and-personality, I would like to propose a new title for our subdiscipline: PSYCHOLOGICAL ANTHROPOLOGY" (Hsu's emphasis; Hsu, 1972, p. 6). A well-known chapter by psychologist D. T. Campbell and anthropologist R. Naroll, "The Mutual Methodological Relevance of Anthropology and Psychology," appeared in that book, thereby helping to solidify this new facet of anthropology (Campbell & Naroll, 1972). That the IACCP and psychological anthropology were essentially christened in 1972 lends further credibility to the idea that the decade of 1970–1979 was central in the development of new emphases in the two disciplines.

6.1.8 Examples of Books Published in the 1970s with Relevant Cultural Content

Berry, J. W. (1976). *Human ecology and cognitive style: Comparative studies in cultural and psychological adaptation.* Published by Sage, this book was instrumental in helping to explain Berry's ecological model that has been instrumental in a large number of cross-cultural research projects.

Brislin, R. W., Lonner, W. J., & Thorndike. R. M. (1973). *Cross-cultural research methods.* Published by Wiley, this was the first text that focused on various methodological issues recognized at the time.

Cole, M., Gay, J., Glick, J. A., & Sharp, D. W. (1971). *The cultural context of learning and thinking.* Published by Basic Books, this text helped solidify Michael Cole's entry into the growing network of cultural psychologists, which included scholars such as Richard Shweder and Clifford Geertz.

Cronbach, L. J., & Drenth, P. J. D. (1972). *Mental tests and cultural adaptation.* Published by Mouton, this edited book was based on a conference by the same title in Istanbul and became one of the most heavily referenced books in the field. It was especially important in development or adaptation of a great variety of psychometric tests.

Levine, R., & Campbell, D. T. (1972). *Ethnocentrsm: Theories of conflict, ethnic attitudes, and group behavior.* Published by Wiley.

Segall, M. H. (1979). *Cross-cultural psychology: Human behavior in global perspective.* Published by Brooks-Cole, this was the first text to provide a general overview of cross-cultural psychology. A paperback book written by Robert Serpell and published in 1976 by Methuen preceded Segall's book, but was not as comprehensive.

Triandis, H. C. (1972). *The analysis of subjective culture.* Published by Wiley.

6.1.9 Book Series

Sensing a growing need for a home for books with themes relating to psychology and culture, in 1975 Sage Publications agreed to publish the series *Cross-Cultural Research and Methodology* (CCRM). It became the first series of its kind, and predated the *Handbook of Cross-Cultural Psychology* (see the next decade). John W. Berry agreed to join me as coeditor. In its 25-year history (it discontinued in 2000), the CCRM was home to more than 25 books featuring various aspects of research and methodology. The most prominent of these texts, originally submitted in 1978 and one of the most frequently cited culture-oriented books ever, was Geert Hofstede's *Culture's Consequences: International Differences in Work-Related Values*. Published in 1980 with the aid of an international and intercultural editorial board, its influence continues. An overview of this book and its influence appears in the next section (1980–1989).

6.1.10 Counseling across Cultures

In 1973, at the annual APA convention in Montreal, there was a symposium that, when viewed historically, became a focal point in the area of cross-cultural counseling (also called culture-centered counseling or multicultural counseling). The symposium, sponsored by the Society for the Psychological Study of Social Issues (Division 9 of the APA), was organized and chaired by the late Paul B. Pedersen of Syracuse University, who was then a visiting professor in the East-West Center's Culture Learning Institute. Among several influential factors that presaged the symposium was a small book, *The Culturally Encapsulated Counselor* (Wrenn, 1962) – yet further evidence that the 1960s was the decade that began to introduce culture as a phenomenon that awakened scholars of many stripes in psychology. Wrenn was a strong supporter of my desire to pursue a PhD at the University of Minnesota, where he became a national figure in counseling psychology.

The APA symposium primarily featured invited psychologists, but also included anthropologists and psychiatrists whose accomplishments in the mental health field were already established. After the session it was decided to include the presentations in a book, resulting in an edited volume, *Counseling across Cultures*, containing 11 chapters (Pedersen, Lonner, & Draguns, 1976) and earning the sobriquet of the "granddaddy" of all subsequent books in the area. The seventh edition of the text, containing 24 chapters, appeared exactly 40 years later (Pedersen, Lonner, Draguns, Trimble, & Sharron del Rio, 2016). The preparation of all seven editions of that book probably ranked second in my career, if measured by the number of hours I devoted to it. By far, my continuous involvement with the JCCP, which has occupied me for half a century, is first, if number of hours is the measure of dedication.

Somewhat curiously, the area of counseling and psychotherapy – counseling and clinical psychology generally – has been noticeably underrepresented in the main artery of cross-cultural and even cultural psychology. Articles in these important areas have been sparse in the JCCP since the very beginning. It is as if these activities lay in the periphery of "pure" scientific cross-cultural psychology, where basic psychological processes, methodological issues, and developmental and social psychological perspectives have tended to dominate both the pages of the JCCP and the scientific program of IACCP conferences. Perhaps these applied specializations are underrepresented in the main thrust of culture-oriented psychology because they have their own popular outlets. Also, counseling psychology may be more of a North American (United States and Canada) enterprise, and therefore has a smaller base of interest. An important book by Gerstein et al. (2009) has helped bridge gaps in this area, where "multicultural" counseling has prevailed. Gerstein et al. assessed counseling from a worldwide perspective. Additionally, the journal *Transcultural Psychiatry*, which grew out of a newsletter and the journal titled *Transcultural Psychiatry Research Review* that was started at Canada's McGill University in 1956, is a popular outlet for articles concerning a wide range of topics in clinical and counseling psychology and psychiatry. Additionally, Culture, Medicine and Psychiatry is an international and interdisciplinary forum for the publication of work in the fields of medical and psychiatric anthropology, cross-cultural psychiatry, and associated cross-societal and clinical epidemiological studies.

6.2 *1980–1989: Arrival of Geert Hofstede and the* Handbook of Cross-Cultural Psychology

The first full decade of the IACCP was greeted by two events that significantly contributed to the growing dynamism of cross-cultural research and scholarship in psychology. Both occurred in 1980, but were preceded by much work in the 1970s. The first event was the publication of the *Handbook of Cross-Cultural Psychology*, and the second was the groundbreaking work of Geert Hofstede. As noted earlier, the *Handbook* had been in a protracted period of development in the mid- to late 1970s. With 1980 as its official date of publication, the decade began with renewed optimism. This six-volume effort marked the first time in the history of psychology that a multivolume set of books was totally devoted to what had recently become the institutionalization of cross-cultural psychology.

6.2.1 The *Handbook*

The titles and coeditors of the six volumes of the HCCP, encompassing 51 chapters, were:

Volume 1, Perspectives: H. C. Triandis and W. W. Lambert
Volume 2, Methodology: H. C. Triandis and J. W. Berry
Volume 3, Basic Processes: H. C. Triandis and W. J. Lonner
Volume 4, Developmental Processes: H. C. Triandis, A. Heron, and
    E. Kroeger
Volume 5, Social Psychology: H. C. Triandis and R. W. Brislin
Volume 6, Psychopathology: H. C. Triandis and J. G. Draguns

As a seminal effort, the *Handbook* became a model for subsequent edited books in the area. For example, the three-volume second edition of the *Handbook* was published in 1997 and is discussed in the section summarizing 1990–1999 activities.

Together with the three-volume second edition of the *Handbook*, these nine books, which amounted to a total of 83 chapters, have easily been the most frequently referenced books in the field. They have been indispensable resources. And with a large number of other books either already published or soon to hit the presses, and a journal that had become established, cross-cultural psychology was becoming rich with bibliographic resources. Other single-volume, edited handbooks have appeared, and I discuss these in due course.

6.2.3 Hofstede: *Culture's Consequences*

The second event that greeted the decade was the publication of Geert Hofstede's *Culture's Consequences: International Differences in Work-Related Values*. This impressive and massive study, initially submitted to Sage Publications in the late 1970s, appeared in 1980 as part of the book series Cross-Cultural Research and Methodology that John Berry and I had introduced in 1975 (see Section 6.1.9). Hofstede's second edition was published in 2001 under the slightly different title, *Culture's Consequences: Comparing Values, Behaviors, and Organizations across Nations*. The Hofstede dimensions, as they have become known, might best be understood in large organizational settings. In their original form they consisted of 1) power distance (a "pecking order" or state of inequality between supervisors and subordinates in organizations), 2) uncertainty avoidance, or the absence of tolerance for ambiguity and the need for rules, 3) individualism-collectivism, or a primary concern for oneself as opposed to a greater concern for the collective, and 4) masculinity-femininity, which contrasted achievement, assertiveness, and specific goals with, instead, a concern for friendliness and getting along with the boss. Some years later, a fifth dimension was added. It was an offshoot of the *Chinese Values Survey*, largely led by Michael Bond (Chinese Culture Connection) (1987). Thus a long-term perspective (thrift, planning, perseverance) was contrasted with a short-term view (respect for tradition, fulfilling social obligations, and saving face). Hofstede's work has been a strong, persistent influence in many facets of culture-oriented psychology.

With a strong formative background in psychological testing and assessment, I continue to have an abiding interest in the ways that psychologists have divvied up the seemingly infinite proclivities of the human mind. This includes intelligence, of course, as well as personality, values, beliefs, interests, attitudes, happiness, psychological disorders, and so on. A common denominator in most of these approaches, certainly including Hofstede's, is the search for patterns that make sense. If patterns are found, descriptions as well as sources of causality may be pinpointed. Culture-oriented psychologists who have a penchant for measuring aspects of the mental labyrinth of the human mind tend to migrate like fireflies to devices that classify, taxonomize, dichotomize, dimensionalize, rank, rate, or otherwise pigeonhole both individuals and the groups (e.g., organizations, cultures, and nation-states) to which they belong. While cross-cultural assessment has a long history (see Cronbach & Drenth, 1972), it tended to gain momentum in the decade of the 1980s and to promote the development of other ways to help explain cultural variations. Key examples are the NEO-PI-R (the "Big Five" or "Five-Factor" inventory; McCrae, Terracciano, et al., 2005), the Schwartz Values Scale (Schwartz, 1992, 2006), various scales designed to measure individualism and collectivism (e.g., Kağıtçıbaşı, 1997; Triandis, 1995,), holistic (Eastern) vs. analytic (Western) thought patterns (Nisbett, 2003), and independent versus interdependent self-construals (Markus & Kitayama, 1991). All of these devices putatively have universal applications and are often used with that in mind (see Lonner, 2011).

6.2.4   A Sabbatical Year in Saarbrücken

During the sixth international IACCP conference in Aberdeen, Scotland, I met Hans-Joachim Kornadt of the University of the Saar, in Saarbrücken, Germany. Learning of my desire to spend a sabbatical year in Germany, he invited me to be a visiting scholar. I looked into it, applied for a professional leave from my university, and also applied for a Fulbright fellowship. I received both, as well as additional financial support from the Deutsche Forschung Gesellschaft (DFG). We spent the 1984–1985 academic year there. My wife (fluent in German) and three children accompanied me, of course, and we lived in a quiet little town not far from Saarbrücken.

Our children went to German schools, where they gained considerable fluency in the language. One of the consequences of that experience was that our middle child, Alyssa, eventually received her PhD in German languages and literature from Washington University in St. Louis. She is currently chair of the department of Russian and German at Wake Forest University (WFU). She and her husband, Hugh, who is a professor of mathematics at WFU, have two daughters.

Things happen. An ugly part of the year found us mired in a fight with the person who was responsible for sub-renting the house we lived in. A series of events largely fueled by misunderstandings (and, we discovered, the paranoid demeanor of our erstwhile landlord) created an atmosphere of mistrust and even threats to our safety. Details are not needed here, but perhaps a rule was learned: if something can go wrong in a foreign country, it probably will. But a second rule prevailed: there is a lot of compassion in the world, and it will eventually win.

While on that combination sabbatical leave/Fulbright, I had the good fortune of meeting Ernest E. Boesch, a noted cultural psychologist who was running the now-defunct Socio-Psychology Research Center whose research centered on Thailand, where Ernest had spent several years as director of a UNESCO initiative on childhood development. The Center was a conveniently short walk from the university. Also present during that period was Stanford University anthropologist Robert Textor, who was one of the initial group of culture trainers for the Peace Corps. The three of us had weekly discussions that featured aspects of our respective culture-oriented disciplines. Ernest and I hit it off so well that for the following three decades we corresponded frequently and visited many times, always at his home. He and his Thai wife, Supanee, were warm and delightful hosts. I played a significant role in his writing a book detailing his Symbolic Action Theory (Boesch, 1991). A capstone of our relationship was the publication of a book that profiled his life and career, and presented a sampling of his writings (Lonner & Hayes, 2007).

My relationship with Boesch also prompted me to penetrate more deeply into the "sister discipline" of cultural psychology – a perspective that I have admired in terms of its methodologies and general approach to understanding the "enigmatic other" – a description Ernest often used to indicate that the typical human being and his or her culture and language is difficult to comprehend. His "seven flaws" commentary on some fundamental differences between cultural and cross-cultural psychology is a classic (Boesch, 1996). I cherish the relationship I had with Ernest. It was a challenge to fathom the way his beautiful and intense mind worked. He was the prototypical polished European scholar, with impressive fluency in four languages. As an additional gift I had the pleasure of spending some time with his second son, Christophe, who has spent nearly his entire career as a primatologist at the Max Planck Institute in Leipzig, where he is director of the department of evolutionary anthropology. Christophe's recent publications and engaging presentations explaining the similarities of chimpanzee and human cultures are available on the institute's website. These accomplishments would have delighted Ernest, who died in 2014 at the age of 98. Ironically, I learned of his death during an IACCP conference in Reims, France.

I convinced Ernest to attend the 1986 IACCP conference in Istanbul. He did so, as a special guest, giving a talk titled "Cultural Psychology in Action-Theoretical Perspective." It was a convenient coincidence that at that conference I began my term as the ninth president of the IACCP, which was an obligatory two-year term, preceded by a two-year term as president-elect.

6.2.5 Introductory Psychology Texts and Culture

One of the psychology students at the University of the Saar was Elke Rump(now Murdock).Shortly after my arrival, Elke expressed an interest in studying in the United States, possibly in a graduate program. I suggested that she consider attending Western Washington University, doing so under the Fulbright program. She applied for and received both admission to the university and student Fulbright status. I was her advisor for two years and also the chair of her master's thesis, the nature of which affected how both of us spent many future hours on a project that had piqued my interest for several years. Because they constitute a bellwether of the discipline, the project focused on the extent to which the authors of 35 introductory psychology texts (IPTs) covered culture. That is, if a given topic was deemed appropriate and currently central to psychological science, it would certainly be noted and perhaps discussed in detail. For instance, all contemporary survey-type IPTs would have to include overviews of human learning and memory, the structure of the senses, the number and nature of mental disorders, and other essential topics comprising the core of the discipline. The extent to which culture and the role it plays in human activity was covered in such texts was the litmus test of inclusion. I discuss this topic in greater detail in the section titled "Teaching Cross-Cultural Psychology."

All authors of the selected texts were American male psychologists who, we hoped, would introduce undergraduate students to the concept of culture and how it fit into the discipline. This analysis was the first time that such an effort was made. Elke received her master's degree and I, as part of my two-year term (1986–1988) as president of the IACCP, reported the results in my presidential address (Lonner, 1989). Hint: Cultural coverage was very slight, and authors who mentioned culture tended to focus on stereotyped and copy-cat findings, such as biased IQ tests, the universality of certain facial expressions of emotions, and the famous Whorf-Sapir hypothesis of linguistic relativity. Twenty years later we conducted a follow-up study using 40 IPTs. We found striking increases in cultural coverage, but with some authors avoiding the topic altogether (Lonner & Murdock, 2008).

6.2.6 Changes in the JCCP's Editorial Advisory Board

Having devoted much time and effort to establish the JCCP, with more than 13 years of focused attention to it, I decided it was time to step down as editor. Based on the premise that others should have an opportunity to sit in the editor's chair, I chose Roy S. Malpass to replace me, doing so because his university at the time, the State University of New York at Plattsburgh, agreed to contribute "in-kind" services such as part-time editorial assistance as well as covering postal expenses incurred in the reviewing of submitted manuscripts. A succession of psychologists followed Malpass, with terms ranging from three to six years. These individuals, chronologically following Malpass, were Juris G. Draguns (Pennsylvania State University), John E. Williams (Wake Forest University), Peter B. Smith (University of Sussex, UK), Fons van de Vijver (Tilburg University), David Matsumoto (San Francisco State University), and, as current editor, Deborah L. Best (Wake Forest University). I stayed on as founding and senior editor, and then changed my title to founding and special issues editor.

Over the years I have shepherded approximately 30 special issues (or special sections). There were also routine changes at the all-important associate editor position. A total of 38 individuals from numerous countries have served in that important slot, and numerous changes were also made at the consulting editor level. Among the most pleasant memories I have after nearly 50 years of involvement with the JCCP and the world of academe has been the collegiality I have had with many devoted scholars. Without their cooperation and dedication, the JCCP would not have survived. There were some bumps and bruises during the half-century, but in general the JCCP has been a big success because of the teams we put together. I take special pride in the fact that the JCCP is the flagship publication of the IACCP and has helped solidify culture's important place in contemporary psychology. It is a beacon to follow in the future.

6.2.7   IACCP Conferences

The 1980s brought five international IACCP conferences at locations throughout the world:

1980: Fifth international IACCP conference. Utkal University, Bhubaneshwar. India. Conference president: Radhanath Rath, India. President-elect: Durganand Sinha, India. Presidential address: none given. J. L. M. Dawson should have given it, but for unknown reasons he did not. Secretary-general: Ype H. Poortinga, The Netherlands. Conference proceedings: *Diversity and Unity in Cross-Cultural Psychology*. R. Rath, H. S. Asthana, D. Sinha, & J. B. P. Sinha, Eds. (Swets & Zeitlinger, 1982).

1982: Sixth international IACCP conference. Aberdeen, Scotland. Conference president: Jan Deregowski, Scotland. President-elect: John W. Berry, Canada. Presidential address: Cross-Cultural Psychology: A View from the Third World. Durganand Sinha, India. Secretary-general: Ype Poortinga, The Netherlands. Conference proceedings: *Expiscations in Cross-Cultural Psychology*. J. B. Deregowski, S. Dziurawiedc, & R. C. Annis, Eds. (Swets & Zeitlinger, 1983).

1984: Seventh international IACCP conference. Mexico City, Mexico. Conference president: Isabel Reyes Lagunes, Mexico. President-elect: Ronald Taft, Australia. Presidential address: Cultural Psychology and Ethnic Psychology: A Comparative Analysis. John W. Berry, Canada. Secretary-general: Ype Poortinga, The Netherlands. Conference proceedings: *From a Different Perspective: Studies of Behavior across Cultures*. I. R. Lagunes & Y. H. Poortinga, Eds. (Swets & Zeitlinger, 1985).

1986: Eighth international IACCP conference. Istanbul, Turkey. Conference president: Çiğdem Kağıtçıbaşı, Turkey. President-elect: Walter J. Lonner, USA. Presidential address: Cross-Cultural Psychology as Psychological Science. Ronald Taft, Australia. Secretary-general: Ruth Munroe, USA. Conference proceedings: *Growth and Progress in Cross-Cultural Psychology*. Ç. Kağıtçıbaşı, Ed. (Swets & Zeitlinger, 1987).

1988: Ninth international IACCP conference. Newcastle, Australia. Conference president: Daphne Keats, Australia. President-elect: Ype Poortinga, The Netherlands. Presidential address: The Introductory Psychology Texts and Cross-Cultural Psychology: Beyond Ekman, Whorf and Biased I.Q. Tests. Walter J. Lonner, USA. Secretary-general: Ruth Munroe, USA. Conference proceedings: *Heterogeneity in Cross-Cultural*

Psychology. D. M. Keats, D. Munro, & L. Mann, Eds. (Swets & Zeitlinger, 1989).

6.3   1990–1999: Reaching a Quarter of a Century

The last decade of the 20th century was the third full decade of institutionalized cross-cultural psychology. The decade began with the first IACCP conference in Japan. The conference took place in beautiful and deer-ridden Nara, Japan's first capital. Following tradition that the IACCP had developed, the International Congress of Psychology, sponsored by the IUPsyS, was held in nearby Kyoto.

The most unique IACCP conference was held in Liege, Belgium, at a venue shared with the Association pour la Recherche Interculturelle (ARIC). The ARIC is a Francophone organization and agreed with the IACCP, an Anglophone organization, to hold their biannual congresses at the same time and location. It was the first formal effort to start an exchange of ideas and promote a dialogue on their shared interest – the psychological study of culture. Unfortunately, it was the one and only joint meeting between these two organizations.[2]

The decade of the 1990s was filled with a variety of developments that reflected strong growth in the area of culture and psychology. Three activities merit comments: 1) inauguration in 1996 of the journal *Culture & Psychology*, 2) publication in 1997 of the second edition of the *Handbook of Cross-Cultural Psychology*, and 3) the 14th international conference of the IACCP, held in 1998.

---

[2] Incidentally, two years earlier, at the IACCP meeting in Australia, there was heated discussion about the JCCP becoming an official bilingual (English and French) journal. There was even some discussion about the IACCP considering a change of its name. I suggested the "International Association for the Psychological Study of Culture (IAPSC)," but it attracted too little attention to merit further thought. The discussion of the JCCP becoming a bilingual journal also gained little traction, for English is the *lingua franca* of science. However, the *International Journal of Psychology* continues to include French abstracts for its articles.

6.3.1   Culture & Psychology

Culture & Psychology is a quarterly peer-reviewed journal that is not affiliated with any association or organization. Published by Sage Publications, its main contributors and readers are cultural psychologists as well as those who primarily identify with cross-cultural psychology, its nearest kin in the psychological study of culture. It does not emphasize empirical papers and by its own description features topics such as "semiotic mediation" and "dialogical nature of the self," and in general focuses on an understanding of the basic psychological makeup of human beings and their intersubjective experiences, emotions, and everyday creativity.

The influential ideas of scholars such as Michael Cole, Clifford Geertz, Richard Shweder, editor Jaan Valsiner, and, of course, the late Ernest Boesch are frequently found in the articles published in *Culture & Psychology*. Now more than 20 years of age, this journal has been a welcome addition to what has become an increasing diversification of the psychological study of culture and the cultural study of psychology.

6.3.2   *Handbook of Cross-Cultural Psychology,* second edition (1997)

As noted earlier, the original six-volume *Handbook of Cross-Cultural Psychology* (Triandis et al., 1980) has frequently been touted as the main effort signaling the institutionalization of cross-cultural psychology. Its initial influence, a decade after the JCCP was inaugurated, can still be felt today.

The editors and titles of the three-volume second edition (Berry et al. 1997) were:

Volume 1: J. W. Berry. Y. H. Poortinga, and J. Pandey, *Theory and Method*
Volume 2: J. W. Berry, P. R. Dasen and T.S. Saraswathi, *Basic Processes and Human Development*
Volume 3: J. W. Berry, M. H. Segall and C. Kagitcibasi, *Social Behavior and Applications*

In all, the three volumes consisted of 34 chapters, 17 fewer than the 51 chapters in the original HCCP.

6.3.3   14th International IACCP Conference

This 1998 conference was noteworthy for two reasons. First, it marked the silver anniversary of the IACCP and was the first IACCP conference held on US soil. Previous conferences were in Hong Kong, Canada (twice), The Netherlands, (then) West Germany, India, Scotland, Mexico, Turkey, Australia, Japan, Belgium, and Spain. The site of the conference, as announced at the 12th international IACCP conference in Pamplona, was originally supposed to be in Bakersfield, California. This is not far from San Francisco, the site of the quadrennial conference of the International Association of Applied Psychology, thus following the tradition of scheduling IACCP conferences within reasonable proximity of the much larger IAAP and IUPsyS congresses. John Berry and I agreed to co-chair the Scientific Committee.

However, six months after the 1994 conference in Pamplona, Spain, I received word from James Georgas, then the secretary-general, that the person who agreed to be the main organizer of the 14th conference withdrew from the agreement because her application for a Fulbright award for the next year was approved. Georgas urged me to assume the responsibility of hosting the conference. I agreed, knowing that it would be a challenge to start six months late. The site of the conference was Western Washington University, and the official host was the Center for Cross-Cultural Research, part of the department of psychology. I put together an organizing team and began work.

The conference was a success. Its 560 registrants set an IACCP attendance record, and also set a record for psychology conferences in the State of Washington in terms of number of registrants from foreign countries. It was also the largest US psychology conference ever north of Seattle, home of the University of Washington. That's not saying much, since Alaska was our only competition! Following tradition, we put together the obligatory volume of selected conference papers (Lonner, Dinnel, Forgays, & Hayes, 1999).

6.3.4 IACCP Conferences

Like the 1980s, the 1990s brought five international IACCP conferences:

1990: Tenth international IACCP conference. Nara, Japan. Conference president: Saburo Iwawaki, Japan. President-elect: Çiğdem Kağıtçıbaşı, Turkey. Presidential address: Toward a Conceptualization of Culture for Psychology. Ype H. Poortinga, The Netherlands. Secretary-general: Ruth H. Munroe, USA. Conference proceedings: *Innovations in Cross-Cultural Psychology*. S. Iwawaki, Y. Kashima, & K. Leung, Eds. (Swets & Zeitlinger, 1992).

1992: Eleventh international IACCP conference. Liege, Belgium. Conference president: Anne-Marie Bouvy, Belgium. President-elect: Roy S. Malpass, USA. Presidential address: Human Development and Societal Development: Linking Theory and Application. Çiğdem Kağıtçıbaşı, Turkey. Secretary-general: Colleen Ward, New Zealand. Conference proceedings: *Journeys into Cross-Cultural Psychology*. A.-M. Bouvy, F. J. R. van de Vijver, P. Boski, & P. Schmitz, Eds. (Swets & Zeitlinger, 1994).

1994: Twelfth international IACCP conference. Pamplona, Spain. Conference president: Hector Grad, Spain. President-elect: Janak Pandey, India. Presidential address: Face Recognition at the Interface of Psychology, Law, and Culture. Roy S. Malpass, USA. Secretary-general: Josephine Naidoo, Canada. Conference proceedings: *Key Issues in Cross-Cultural Psychology*. H. Grad, A. Blanco, & J. Georgas, Eds. (Taylor & Francis, 1996).

1996: Thirteenth international IACCP conference. Montreal, Canada. Conference president: J.-C. Lasry, Canada. President-elect: Marshall H. Segall, USA. Presidential address: Socio-Cultural Dimensions of Experience and Consequences of Crowding. Janak J. B. Pandey, India. Secretary-general: James Georgas, Greece. Conference proceedings: *Latest Contributions to Cross-Cultural Psychology*. J. G. Adair, J.-C. Lasry, & K. L. Dion, Eds. (Taylor & Francis, 1999).

1998: Fourteenth international IACCP conference. Western Washington University, Bellingham, Washington, USA. Conference president: Walter J. Lonner, USA. President-elect: Michael H. Bond, Hong Kong. Presidential address: Why Is There Still Racism if There Is No Such Thing as Race? Marshall H. Segal, USA. Secretary-general: James Georgas, Greece. Conference proceedings: *Merging Past, Present and Future in Cross-Cultural Psychology.* W. J. Lonner, D. L. Dinnel, D. K. Forgays, & S. A. Hayes, Eds. (Swets & Zeitlinger, 1999).

6.4 2000–2009: A Major Change and New Developments

The turn of the century and the beginning years of the fourth decade of activities involving the IACCP–JCCP coalition brought forth a number of significant happenings. These included the ongoing international conferences and development of new programs devoted to cultural studies. Perhaps the most important development was a radical change in operation of the JCCP. For nearly 35 years I had had virtually complete control of the JCCP, which was the main activity of the Center for Cross-Cultural Research. For 30 of those years, the IACCP–JCCP coalition ran smoothly. A succession of editors who followed me received a modicum of financial support in the form of quarterly stipends. A requirement of their appreciated and productive editorships was that the universities for which they worked agreed to help the operation by contributing work-in-kind support. This support came in the form of secretarial assistance, payment of occasional travel expenses, and sometimes reduced teaching loads. I continued my unbroken involvement with the JCCP, and of course continued full-time teaching until I retired in 2001.

Over the years I managed to oversee a sizeable balance in a JCCP account sufficient for me to attend conferences and provide some funds for activities benefiting instruction and related activities at Western Washington University. For example, I invited a number of scholars to the campus at no expense to the university. Most importantly, through royalties from Sage and an effective editorial board, I was able to coordinate the smooth running of the JCCP.

6.4.1 The Game Changer

In 2003, at a regional IACCP conference in Budapest, a senior acquisitions editor from Sage Publications offered a proposal: Sage, which at the time had been publishing the JCCP for 30 years, wished to purchase the JCCP copyright from Western. The offer was a total surprise, and the amount Sage initially suggested was staggering, considering our modest beginnings.

When I returned home I explained the offer to Western officials whose purview and responsibilities included such matters. They viewed the JCCP copyright as a commodity owned by the State of Washington and therefore for sale at the right price, and the offer was especially attractive to a state university that always seemed to be strapped for money. The sale was consummated on May 5, 2004 during a short meeting in the president's office. For 15 seconds I held the Sage check of $1.25 million in my hands. Additionally, the final arrangement included splitting the annual royalties that were set at 14%. Over the roughly 16 years since the sale, this has amounted to a per annum average of about $60,000 for both the CCCR and the IACCP. Prior to the sale the IACCP had had little cash in its treasury. Over the past 16 years, the IACCP has received roughly $1,200,000 from the takeover, thus giving the association the funds to do a number of creative and helpful things. Many students have benefited from this transaction, and the association, under the authority of its Communications and Publications Committee, retained control of the scholarly and editorial aspect of the JCCP. Compared with the early days, when 15-hour days and scraping for help were common, this was a gigantic change.

The Sage transaction came with strongly conflicting consequences. On one hand, I lost control of "my baby" (an endearment I enjoyed using), but on the other, it greatly improved the association's flexibility. It was finally able to do many things that required funding. Among the first actions it took was to create the Walter J. Lonner Distinguished Invited Lecture Series that was to be featured at future IACCP conferences. Chosen to give the inaugural lecture in 2006 was the late Gustav Jahoda, the IACCP's first full-term president. Five additional invited speakers have been chosen in as many international IACCP (even year) conferences. The IACCP agreed that future speakers chosen for the Lonner lectures should be scholars from collateral fields, and not from the large number of IACCP regulars. Sandra Jovchelovitch of the London School of Economics recently accepted an invitation to be the seventh speaker in the ongoing series. The names of these speakers and the titles of their lectures appear later, in the synopses of the conferences.

6.4.2   A New Centre

In 2004, the year of the sale of the copyright, the School of Psychology at Victoria University in Wellington, New Zealand established the Centre for Applied Cross-Cultural Research (CACR). To a large extent this new entity used the Center for Cross-Cultural Research (CCCR) at Western Washington University as a model for its activities. Focusing largely on globalization and migration, its broader goal was to understand differences and similarities, accept and enhance cultural diversity, and to enhance intercultural relations.

Desiring closer contacts with like-minded organizations and centers such as the CACR, I brokered a memorandum of understanding (MOU) between the CCCR and the CACR. It was a natural thing to do, especially since I had already been invited to the CACR twice as a visiting professor. This arrangement was to involve short-term exchanges of faculty and students in an effort to build bridges and cooperate in mutually acceptable research projects. The funds were certainly available. The appropriate officials at both universities signed the MOU but unfortunately nothing came of it.

6.4.3   Additional Activities in the Decade

The first decade of the 21st century witnessed a number of initiatives and projects that bolstered the resources available to culture-oriented psychologists. The two major activities were the *Online Readings in Psychology and Culture*, and the beginnings of the IACCP archives.

6.4.4   *Online Readings in Psychology and Culture*

I taught my undergraduate course, Psychology and Culture, for 35 years. The few texts routinely available for the first 20 years were helpful, especially if accompanied by selected readings such as journal articles and chapters from selected books. Eventually finding that approach unacceptable, in 1990 I decided to put together a book of original invited readings authored by selected culture-oriented scholars. I invited Roy S. Malpass to join me as coeditor, and the book, *Psychology and Culture* (Lonner & Malpass, 1994), contained 43 chapters arranged in seven sections. The book served the intended purpose quite well, and was used internationally. After several years, altered priorities prevented a second edition. Disappointed but not deterred, I began plans for a similar but much more expansive project. Thus, the *Online Readings in Psychology and Culture* (ORPC) was launched.

The ORPC was guided by the principle of "giving cross-cultural psychology away," a phrase partially borrowed from George A. Miller's APA presidential address in 1969 (see the Introduction of this Element). I reasoned that there were many hundreds of scholars throughout the world who had plenty of important things to say about the influence of culture on a broad range of psychological topics. They merely had to put pen to paper and write it. I also reasoned that this collective power should be put to use. Furthermore, and most importantly, the advent of cyberspace and especially the Internet could be used effectively to reach scholars and students around the world by providing free readings. The ORPC was inaugurated in 2001, the year I retired, and was copyrighted by Western Washington University.

A few years later, it became clear that no active member on the Western faculty wanted to sustain the ORPC in some kind of editorial or proprietary capacity. I then insisted that Western relinquish the copyright of this not-for-profit effort and transfer it forthright to the IACCP. Because the ORPC was explicitly designed to enhance the teaching of cross-cultural psychology, it was fitting that the IACCP take control, which it gladly did. It is now one of four official publications associated with the IACCP, the others being the JCCP, the *Cross-Cultural Psychology Bulletin*, and the volumes comprising selected proceedings of IACCP conferences. The small ORPC editorial team currently consists of Wolfgang Friedlmeier (the United States and Germany), Michael Bender (The Netherlands), Chuck Hill (the United States), and me. It has been a pleasure to work with them on this important mainstay of IACCP offerings.

We continue to believe that the ORPC, which now numbers about 110 readings, is an effective way to inform students around the world. It is a unique contribution to the field. Many psychology instructors, especially in institutions with limited financial resources, use the ORPC as the only "text." In December 2017, downloads of ORPC articles exceeded the 1 million mark – surely some kind of record. It is especially heartwarming to know that the ORPC is reaching so many students and scholars who may be unable to afford expensive books sold by many commercial publishers. Readers of the Elements in Psychology and Culture series may want to contribute to the ORPC. Details can be found at IACCP.org.

6.4.5 The IACCP Archives

During the 18th international IACCP conference in Spetses, Greece (2006), John Berry and I outlined a plan to initiate the IACCP Archives Project. We thought the Association had been around long enough to generate much material worth saving for posterity, and that we should develop plans to do so. Items of historical interest include minutes of general assembly reports, reports of IACCP conferences, correspondence generated by the activities of members of the Executive Council, books containing selected readings from conferences, all copies of the JCCP and the *Cross-Cultural Psychology Bulletin*, significant developments, and so on. The IACCP endorsed the idea and encouraged those involved (mainly Berry and me) to continue looking into the matter.

The major problem focused on who would collect the material and where the archives should be stored and maintained. We considered a few universities as candidates for the home of the archives because of their prior involvement in early stages of organized cross-cultural psychology. However, none of the prime candidates, including Western Washington University, exhibited much interest because of the costs involved and the disinterest of current faculty members whose interests in archival material were tepid, at best. Eventually we found an excellent solution. The Cummings Center for the History of Psychology (CCHP), associated with the University of Akron's (Ohio) department of psychology, contracted with the IACCP to house and maintain the archives. The ongoing project will be coordinated by the Communications and Publications Committee of the IACCP. More developments along these lines are expected.

6.4.6   The Conferences

Continuing the established pattern, the new decade brought a series of international IACCP conferences:

2000: Fifteenth international IACCP conference. Pultusk School of Humanities, Pultusk, Poland. Conference president: Pawel Boski, Poland. President-elect: Deborah L. Best, USA. Presidential address: You and the IACCP: Some Social Psychological Reflections on Organizational Homebuilding. M. H. Bond, Hong Kong. Secretary-general: Klaus Boehnke, Germany. Conference proceedings: New Directions in Cross-Cultural Psychology. P. Boski, F. J. R. van de Vijver, & A. M. Chodynicka, Eds. (Polish Psychological Association, 2002).

2002: Sixteenth international IACCP conference. Yogyakarta, Indonesia. Conference president: Bernadette N. Setiadi. President-elect: Peter B. Smith, England. Presidential address:

Deborah L. Best: Robber's Cave Revisited: Lessons for Cross-Cultural Psychology. Secretary-general: Klaus Boehnke, Germany. Conference proceedings: *Ongoing Themes in Psychology and Culture.* B. Setiadi, A. Supratiknya, W. Lonner, & Y. Poortinga, Eds. (Kanisius, 2004).

2004: Seventeenth international IACCP conference. Xi'an, China. Conference president: Gang Zheng, China. President-elect: Shalom Schwartz, Israel. Presidential address: Who Are We, Where Do We Come From, and Where Are We Going? Peter B. Smith, England. Secretary-general: Klaus Boehnke, Germany. Conference proceedings: *Perspectives and Progress in Contemporary Cross-Cultural Psychology.* Z. Gang, K. Leung, & J. G. Adair, Eds. (China Light Industry Press, 2007).

2006: Eighteenth international IACCP conference. Spetses, Greece. Conference president: Aikaterini Gari and Kostas Mylonas, Greece. President-elect: James Georgas, Greece. Presidential address: Causes of Culture: National Differences in Cultural Embeddedness. Shalom Schwartz, Israel. Secretary-general: Klaus Boehnke, Germany. Conference proceedings: *Quad erat demonstrandum: From Herodotus' Ethnographic Journeys to Cross-Cultural Research.* A. Gari & K. Mylonas, Eds. (Pedio Books, 2009). Lonner Lecture: Reflections on Two of Our Early Ancestors. Gustav Jahoda, Scotland.

2008: Nineteenth international IACCP conference. Jacobs University, Bremen, Germany. Conference president: William K. Gabrenya Jr., USA. President-elect: Heidi Keller, Germany. Presidential address: How Different and Similar Are Families across Cultures? A 30 Nation Psychological Study. James Georgas, Greece. Secretary-general: William K. Gabrenya Jr., USA. Conference proceedings: *Rendering Borders Obsolete: Cross-Cultural and Cultural Psychology as an Interdisciplinary, Multi-Method Endeavor.* F. Deutsch, M. Boehnke, U. Kühnen, & K. Boehnke, Eds. (International Association for Cross-Cultural Psychology, 2011). Lonner Lecture: The Human Adaptation for Culture. Michael Tomasello, Germany/USA.

6.5 2010–2019: Reaching Half a Century

The current decade is nearly over, with just one international IACCP conference, the 24th, remaining as I write this in December 2017 – the 2018 conference in Guelph (see later in this volume). It is likely that the 2020 conference will be held in Olomouc, a city near the center of the Czech Republic, and that Tokyo will be the venue for the 2022 conference. The conference in 2020 will have special significance because it will be the 25th biennial conference and thus the 50th anniversary of the IACCP. And this year – 2018 – is the 50th anniversary of my joining the Western faculty. As explained earlier, it will also be the 50th anniversary of my getting the green light to make plans leading to the launch of the JCCP.

6.5.1 The International Conferences

2010: Twentieth international IACCP conference. Melbourne, Australia. Conference president: Amanda Gordon, Australia. President-elect: Kwok Leung, Hong Kong. Presidential address: Future Perspectives for Cross-Cultural Psychology: Some Considerations of a Developmental Psychologist. Heidi Keller, Germany. Secretary-general: William K. Gabrenya Jr. USA. Conference proceedings: *Steering the Cultural Dynamics.* Y. Kashima, E. Kashima, & R. Beatson, Eds. (International Association for Cross-Cultural Psychology, 2013). Lonner Lecture: Lawrence Harrison, USA. Untitled talk.

2012: Twenty-first international IACCP conference. Stellenbosch, South Africa. Conference president: Deon Meiring and Leon Jackson, South Africa. President-elect: Yoshihisa Kashima, Australia. Presidential address: The Role of Indigenous Research in Constructing Universal Theories. Kwok Leung, Hong Kong. Secretary-general: William K. Gabrenya Jr., USA. Conference proceedings: *Toward Sustainable Development through Nurturing Diversity.* L. Jackson, D. Meiring, F. J. R. van de Vijver, E. Idemudia, & W. Gabrenya, Eds. (International

Association for Cross-Cultural Psychology, 2014). Lonner Lecture: Religious and Sacred Imperatives in Human Conflict. Scott Atran, France/USA.

2014: Twenty-second international IACCP conference. Reims, France. Conference president: Christine Roland-Lévy, France. President-elect: Patricia Greenfield, USA. Presidential address: Yoshihisa Kashima, Australia. Secretary-general: William Gabrenya Jr., USA. Conference proceedings: *Unity, Diversity and Culture.* C. Roland-Lévy, P. Denoux, B. Voyer, P. Boski, & W. Gabrenya, Eds. (International Association for Cross-Cultural Psychology, 2016). Lonner Lecture: On the Role of Culture in the Emergence of Language. Daniel Everett, USA.

2016: Twenty-third international IACCP conference. Nagoya, Japan. Conference president: Minoru Karasawa, Japan. President-elect: Fons van de Vijver, The Netherlands. Presidential address: Social Changes, Cultural Education, and Human Development: United States, China, and Japan. Patricia Greenfield, USA. Secretary-general: Marta Fulop, Hungary. Conference proceedings: Lonner Lecture: Embodiment and Enactment in Cultural Psychiatry: From Neurophenomenology to Situated Practice. Laurence J. Kirmayer, Canada.

2018: Twenty-fourth international IACCP conference. Guelph University, Guelph, Canada. Conference president: Saba Safdar, Canada. President-elect: Klaus Boehnke, Germany. Presidential address: Fons van de Vijver. Secretary-general: Marta Fulop, Hungary. Lonner Lecture: Human Development and Contextual Adversity: Role and Resources of Culture. Sandra Jovchelovitch, United Kingdom.

2020: Twenty-fifth international IACCP conference. The golden anniversary conference will likely be held in Olomouc, Czech Republic. Please see IACCP.org for details and possible changes.

6.5.2 Regional IACCP Conferences

As noted earlier, the IACCP decided at the outset to hold its biennial international conferences in even-numbered years and its regional conferences in odd-numbered years, and in close geographic proximity to the IAAP and IUPsyS conferences, both of which are held quadrennially. For further information about these conferences, see IACCP.org. The dates and locations of the smaller conferences are as follows:

1973	Ibadan, Nigeria
1975, 1977, and 1979	– No regional conferences on record
1981	Asian Regional, Taipei, Taiwan (with the International Council of Psychologists)
1983	Asian Regional, Kuala Lumpur, Malaysia
1985	European Regional, Malmo, Sweden
1987	North American Regional, Kingston, Canada
1989	European Regional, Amsterdam, Netherlands
1991	European Regional, Debrecen, Hungary
1992	Fourth Asian Regional Conference, Kathmandu, Nepal (January 2–4)
1995	Asia Pacific Regional, Guangzhou (in collaboration with the IUPsyS and the IAAP)
1995	African regional, Obafemi Awolowo University, Ile-Ife, Osun State, Nigeria
1996	II Regional congress of IACCP, Hermosillo, October 23–25, 1996
1999	1999 Regional Congress of IACCP on Cultural Diversity and European Integration, jointly organized with the International Test Commission
2001	Fifth European Regional, Winchester, UK
2003	European Regional, Budapest, Hungary
2005	European regional, San Sebastian, Spain
2007	Mexico City, Mexico
2009	Africa Regional, University of Buea, Cameroon
2011	European Regional, Istanbul Turkey
2013	North American Regional, Los Angeles, USA
2015	San Cristóbal de las Casas, Chiapas, Mexico

7 Two Final Topics: Methodological Perspectives and the Teaching of Culture and Psychology

So far in this Element I have summarized a number of developments in cross-cultural psychology that I and a host of colleagues have witnessed and in which I have actively participated. But no treatment of the history and scope of cross-cultural psychology – even a brief one such as this – can be complete without giving overviews of two exceptionally important topics. The first topic concerns methodological concepts, procedures, and issues. Following that is the pedagogical matter of teaching cross-cultural psychology.

7.1 Methodological Considerations: Key Concepts in a Nutshell

As a science, psychology is bound to follow the canons of established scientific principles and procedures. Cross-cultural psychology, the vast majority of which is either explicitly or implicitly culture-comparative, is not exempt from the requirements demanded of those engaged in scientific inquiry. The main difference between orthodox and routine research in psychology and its culture-comparative component is the entrance of a rather tricky set of circumstances and issues that require serious attention. Some have argued that cross-cultural psychology is not a *subfield* in the discipline but is actually a *special method of inquiry* with its own particular array of circumstances and issues that need to be addressed.

7.1.1 Etics and Emics

The so-called etic-emic dilemma provides a time-honored array of these circumstances and issues. The dilemma was introduced by psycholinguist Kenneth Pike in 1954, and is often referred to as the "Insider-Outsider Debate" that has been a central concept in a variety of disciplines (see Pike, 1967). Berry (1969) included the concept as part of the early challenges facing the nascent establishment of organized cross-cultural psychology. In culture-comparative psychology, the essence of the "debate," which is more instructive and orienting than divisive, is whether universals (etics) and cultural specifics (emics) can "get together" and make sense while explaining thought and behavior across different systems of meaning (cultures). The essence of this methodological conundrum is whether any chosen psychological construct can serve as a guiding template when conducting research in other cultures, and why or why not. For example, can research on personality, which almost always includes some psychometric device (see Allik, et al., 2017; Allik & McCrae, 2004), be uncritically imposed on cultures where research on personality using extraneous measures is totally foreign?

This process of extending the range of (possible or presumed) variation of psychological phenomena is central to culture-comparative research. For decades cross-cultural psychologists have been drawn to a wide assortment of devices designed to measure personality, values, attitudes, interests, and other human characteristics. The primary motive in these efforts has been to find patterns, facets, dimensions, and various taxonomies that help to describe and explain behavior in other cultures (see Lonner, 2011). Summaries of the emic-etic problem and its consequences and possible solutions appear in numerous places, including Keith's (2013) *Encyclopedia of Cross-Cultural Psychology*.

Additional philosophical and scientific debate includes a trio of "isms" – Absolutism, Relativism, and Universalism. Consider two simple questions, each to be answered "Yes" or "No": 1) Should commonalities in human behavior be assumed and emphasized in research? 2) Should specific cultural contexts guide all culture-oriented research? An Absolutist would answer "Yes" to the first question and "No" to the second, and for a Relativist the answers would be reversed. The Universalist would answer in the affirmative to both questions. And, as Adamopoulos and Lonner (1994) pointed out, answering "No" to both questions would suggest something like scientific nihilism. Fontaine (2013) discussed further methodological considerations.

7.1.2   Psychological Universals versus Cultural Relativism

The protracted discussion of psychological universals as opposed to cultural relativism is another important topic in cross-cultural methodology. The topic centers around a fundamental question that begets other questions: Are there universals (beyond yawning truisms such as "all people breathe, eat, and sleep") that can be used to form a consistent comparative base? If so, what are they, how does one know they exist, and why is it necessary to establish their existence in culture-comparative research? Among other discussions of psychological universals, four presentations of the topic, in chronological order, are Aberle et al. (1950), Lonner (1980), Brown (1991), and Norenzayan and Heine (2005). The latter two references are especially informative.

The position of "radical cultural relativism" has sometimes been used to characterize psychologists who favor hermeneutics and deep cultural immersion over the routine quantitative methods often favored by many cross-cultural researchers. Historically, there has been a tendency to favor one over the other. The content of the two leading journals in these approaches – *Culture and Psychology* and the JCCP – generally attests to this distinction. A well-known quote by the late anthropologist Clifford Geertz (1973) fuels the fear that the core of any culture is too complex to promote anything but extremely deep excursions into the labyrinth:

> Cultural analysis is intrinsically incomplete. And, worse than that, the more deeply it goes the more incomplete it is (p. 29).

7.1.3   One Planet, Many Lenses

However, the seemingly divisive nature of a simple dichotomy of qualitative (cultural psychology) versus quantitative (cross-cultural psychology) has worn thin because frequently the hats change. Culture-oriented psychologists are now part of a multifaceted assortment of perspectives that were discussed during a symposium at the 2014 IACCP conference in Reims,

France (see Lonner, 2016). These perspectives are vying for pulpits from which to preach their own form of the gospel – cultural psychology, cross-cultural psychology, indigenous psychology, ethnic psychology, and psychological anthropology – to name the more prominent ones. It has become quite difficult at times to tell with which culture-focused orientation the author of a contemporary book or journal article identifies. We are now in a "Big Tent" era that makes it difficult to discern one methodological preference over another (see later in this volume for additional comments on this symposium).

7.1.4   Bias and Equivalence

An additional methodological area that is often problematic concerns the issues of bias and equivalence.in testing, assessment, and other methods used to measure any attribute for comparative study. Bias and equivalence are two sides of the same coin: the lack of equivalence points to bias, and the establishment of equivalence eliminates bias. There are numerous types of bias that can seriously affect equivalence in culture-comparative research. This is a brief list of biases that could taint or skew results:

> Construct bias: Does a construct (e.g., hedonism) have the same meaning in the cultures being studied?
>
> Method, experience, and procedural bias: Differences between individuals or groups in their exposure to various methods used in psychological research
>
> Linguistic (or translation) bias: Non-uniformity in written or spoken questions or instructions in taking tests, completing surveys, or responding to questions
>
> Scalar, or full-score comparability bias: Are the scales of measurement used in two or more groups based on the same ratios (the "apples to oranges" analogy)?

A multipurpose overview such as this cannot cover in suitable detail all of the methodological issues and problems that researchers must carefully consider in all projects designed to gather data and information from individuals with different life experiences.

Of course, this is true in all psychological research. The difficulties are compounded when cultural boundaries are crossed. For starters, I recommend consulting a chronological presentation of methods used in cross-cultural research. Brislin, Lonner, and Thorndike (1973) made an initial attempt to provide methodological guidelines. Their work was followed, in order, by Triandis et al. (1980); Lonner and Berry (1986); Berry, Poortinga, and Pandey (1997); van de Vijver and Leung (1997); Greenfield, 2000; Matsumoto and Yoo (2006); van de Vijver (2009); Fontaine (2011); Matsumoto and van de Vijver (2011); and Fischer and Poortinga (in press). The latter is a special issue of the JCCP that calls for increasing care in cross-cultural research methodology. I realize this would be a lot of reading, but the serous and assiduous scholar/researcher will want to do it right, and the only way to achieve that is to read and absorb the cautions and recommendations that have accumulated over the years.

7.2 Teaching Cross-Cultural Psychology

Until about 1970, psychology departments in the United States (and almost certainly everywhere else) did not offer routine classes or courses of study that featured culture. This widespread inattention to such an enormous mediator and moderator of human behavior slowly ended when, as I have described throughout this Element various events led to the still-increasing institutionalization and globalization of the discipline. The first such course with which I was involved carried a cumbersome title: "The Cultural Conditioning of Psychological Phenomena." I co-taught it twice with Bob Meade during the 1969–1970 academic year. About six graduate students enrolled in this three-credit elective course. We had no text because none deemed appropriate was available. We found some relevant journal articles, but primarily used our own experiences and ideas about course content in our seminar-style class.

The pedagogical situation started to improve in 1970, the year that the JCCP was launched. And when the IACCP was inaugurated in 1972 the way or ways that culture was handled in psychology curricula changed radically. From then on, I and a growing number of colleagues taught courses in the area. I taught my own undergraduate course, Psychology and Culture, more than 100 times during my career, and even taught it several times after I retired in 2001. The classes were always full (enrollment was limited to room size), and on several occasions more than 150 students took it. (At Western Washington University that was a very large class.) I also taught an upper-division undergraduate "Seminar in Cross-Cultural Psychology" as well as a graduate "Seminar in Cross-Cultural Counseling." The latter was, and remains, a required course in both the Mental Health Counseling and School Counseling curricula at Western.

Tempting as it was, and is, to attribute the popularity of these courses to my skills or abilities in the classroom, I believe that students were attracted to them because the perilous world was changing and the students yearned for new and exciting things. After all, the psychology department at (then) Western Washington State College had curricular offerings that were generally packaged and treated as "real" psychology, led by faculty members who had generally received doctorates in traditional "hard-core" experimental programs. Anything unorthodox or "new" was suspect, and was a candidate for scorn or even ridicule. "Old-timers" with interests in psychology and culture can regale contemporary students with stories about their being part of the "lunatic fringe" of the discipline. Culture-oriented psychologists were often at the bottom of the food chain, and were sometimes chided for wasting time in areas that many thought belonged to anthropologists. Just as often, anthropologists were prone to criticize psychologists who encroached on culture, their coveted private domain. That was certainly true at Western, but it no longer holds true. The general consensus is that anthropology and psychology need each other. I have always encouraged students to study anthropology as well as other languages. Fortunately, the department chair at the time, the late Merle E. Meyer, was comfortably egalitarian despite his strong background in experimental psychology. As I pointed out earlier, the JCCP may not have been launched – at least not at Western – without Meyer's encouragement or the rare window of opportunity that opened in the late 1960s.

My own experience with pecking-order mentality occurred in 1969, shortly after I cofounded the Center for Cross-Cultural Research. I was assigned one of a nest of five offices in a recently extended and renovated building that housed the department of psychology. The appropriate campus facility affixed the full title of the Center on the glass door leading to the inner suite of offices. Soon after the painting was completed, a member of the department drew a line through the "cross" part and above it, with a grease pencil, inserted the word "Horti-," thereby in a juvenile act of academic bullying renaming our unit the "Center for Horti-Cultural Research." I knew who did it, but never gave him the pleasure of confrontation and rarely mentioned it to anyone. Fortunately, most of the other 25 faculty members were supportive of this innovation, some of them enthusiastically. I enjoyed what I was doing, worked hard at it while exercising my rights under the yoke of academic freedom, earned respect from many friends on campus, and generally was thankful that Western hired a person with such a spotty previous decade of wandering, wondering, and wayfaring.

By the mid-1970s the inclusion of culture in psychology curricula was becoming increasingly common in many countries. Numerous books appeared, with scholars such as Harry Triandis, John Berry, Ype Poortinga, Gustav Jahoda, and Marshall Segall (among many others) contributing texts specifically written for courses of study that focused on culture's influence on human thought and behavior. When the calendar rolled over to the 1980s, academic psychologists who developed culture-oriented courses had a small avalanche of texts and journal articles from which to choose. The publication of the six-volume *Handbook of Cross-Cultural Psychology* in 1980 became instrumental in psychology education, and its three-volume second edition, edited by Berry et al. and published in 1997, continued to influence the teaching of psychology. Other culture-oriented handbooks and books of readings were becoming increasingly popular. By the turn of the century, culture-oriented psychologists enjoyed a feast of books and other resources that enriched their teaching. For instance, the *Handbook of Culture and Psychology* (Matsumoto, 2001) and its revision (Matsumoto & Hwang, in press) helped carry the torch even further. This *Handbook* includes several chapters written to help academic psychologists orient their courses. One such chapter gives a broad overview of topics and resources – too numerous to discuss here – in the areas of psychology that feature culture (Lonner et al., in press). A four-volume collection of readings was a welcome addition (Smith & Best, 2009), and the three-volume *Encyclopedia of Cross-Cultural Psychology* (Keith, 2013) is a valuable resource. The *Encyclopedia* contains biographical sketches of prominent scholars, past and present, in the field as well as overviews of concepts and topics employed in various research orientations. Psychology educators, especially those whose responsibilities include undergraduate education, may also benefit from assessing and monitoring how culture and its related concepts are handled in introductory psychology texts (IPTs), a topic I discuss in the next section.

7.2.1   Introductory Psychological Texts (IPTs)
Neither local (countrywide) nor international data systematically summarizing curricular offerings in the area of psychology and culture appear to be currently available. But the situation is certainly changing. There are data, however, on the inclusion of culture in ubiquitous introductory psychology texts (IPTs).

7.2.2   Introductory Textbooks
A relatively recent comparison of such content in IPTs over a 20-year span (Lonner, 1989; Lonner & Murdock, 2008) showed a striking, but quite varied, increase in the cultural content of the most widely used IPTs in undergraduate education. Scott and Safdar (2016) presented similar comparative data for recent social psychology texts in Canada. Divisions 2 (Teaching of Psychology) and 52

(International Psychology) of the APA have been active in recent years in the promotion and teaching of culture-oriented perspectives (e.g., Keith, 2018; Lonner, 2015). In 2018 a conversation hour on this topic was on the program of the APA's annual convention in San Francisco. The session, cosponsored by Divisions 2 and 52 and chaired by Ken Keith (past president of Division 2), featured David Myers, the author of best-selling IPTs, and myself. It is through efforts like these that the cultural content of IPTs will continue to improve.

Over the years and peaking in the mid-1980s, I became increasingly concerned about the coverage of culture in the basic texts required of students taking the introductory course. Institutionalized cross-cultural psychology was by then about 15 years old, and hundreds of books, monographs, and journal articles were readily available. Were the authors of IPTs taking advantage of these expanding resources? Were these materials trickling down to the millions of students, many of whom would eventually become psychology teachers and also enter careers in other branches of psychology? In general, were the various approaches to study culture that had been engineered by psychologists in many countries taking hold?

In my IACCP presidential address (Lonner, 1989) I listed several reasons for the surprising lack of cultural content in IPTs written in the mid-1980s. Summarized, with added contemporary commentaries, the reasons were:

1. The authors of IPTs may believe in the essential validity and generalizability of nearly all psychological theories, research, and applications. This would be tantamount to bowing to absolutism. Comment: Why not challenge students by suggesting alternative ways to think about what has been done in the past? Why not open doors for students who absolutely must toil in an increasingly globalized world?
2. It is difficult enough to explain behavior in one's own culture, let alone in other cultures. Why complicate things by adding a cultural dimension? Comment: Adding the cultural dimension

would likely elucidate the situation, not complicate it. Cultures and their ways of dealing with the world add plausible rival hypotheses regarding a great variety of conditions and situations.

3. Authors may feel there is insufficient room in IPTs for anything beyond the basics. Psychology is a huge field, and any attempt to cover everything would result in either failure or a gigantic text that few students could afford and no one would want to publish. Comment: Although this may be true, creative authors should make an effort to at least summarize the intent of culture-oriented psychologists. Numerous IPT authors have done this, and more will continue along those lines.

4. Most authors of IPTs may consider themselves insufficiently familiar with other cultures and ethnic groups to do an adequate job. Moreover, they may not be familiar with the kind of literature that would be appropriate. Many may assume that other academic areas, primarily anthropology, are responsible for educating students about culture. Comment: With so many more resources available than there were 30 years ago, it would be much easier to do this now. Show me the person who understands many of the complexities of life in foreign places and I will show you an educated person.

5. Most students may be so unfamiliar with the broader world that they do not have the constructs necessary to assimilate and accommodate the magnificent array of cultures and the way they work. Therefore, many authors may choose to ignore such material and instead aim for the attention of the lowest common denominator of understanding. Comment: This would be a wonderful opportunity to stimulate any cognitive activity that would improve accommodation and assimilation.

One or more of these explanations, or selected parts of all of them, may still be true in some quarters. However, making beginning students aware of the many current ways that psychology, as an important discipline, has contributed to understanding how the world works is a critical part of education. Ignoring the wealth of information now available would be a grave mistake, and even worse, maintaining cultural stereotypes or failing to challenge assumptions many people make when discussing "the other" would be a tragedy.

Nearly 30 years have passed since the initial textbook study (Lonner, 1989), and more than 10 years since the updated analysis. It is time for an updated study. Should anyone care to engage in a follow-up study, it would be important to decide on procedures to be used. Three approaches to assessing the cultural content of any basic text in psychology are 1) impressionistic and qualitative, 2) strictly quantitative, and 3) some mixture of the two. The first approach (impressionistic/qualitative) is easily the most common: the instructor (or committee) in search of a text simply checks the table of contents and the indexes, and thumbs through the text to gain an impression. The quantitative approach typically relies on word count, whereby the number of words dealing with culture in each chapter, for example, is expressed as a fraction of the total. Thus, the sum of the fractions for all chapters is an index of cultural "density." Griggs and his colleagues have used this method extensively (see Griggs & Jackson, 2013). Word counts are attractive because they satisfy the quest for exactitude and empirical reproducibility. But word counts say nothing about the *quality* of the topic embedded in the word count, unless one assumes that anything of poor quality would not have been chosen by the authors of the texts.

The third method (combined qualitative/quantitative) is the one that Murdock and I considered best because it satisfied our purposes. We used a letter-grading system that identified either *lines of text* for Grades A and B, and *word count* for Grades C, D, and E, as well as our own evaluation of the quality of each cultural "hit." It therefore contains elements of both quantitative and qualitative approaches. This system requires a substantial degree of familiarity with contemporary culture-oriented research. Our independent evaluations (both of us had copies of all the texts; I was at my home in Bellingham, Washington and she was in Luxembourg) were similar, and never differed by one letter grade, and we quickly resolved our rare differences. If anyone should do a follow-up study, we recommend using our procedure because it is clear and easily replicable. We were, of course, only looking for an appropriate way to gauge changes in content over time. We were not engaged in a psychological experiment.

7.2.3 Specialized Materials

A number of specialty texts that provide overviews of culture-oriented psychology are available (e.g., Berry, Poortinga, Breugelmans, Chasiotis, & Sam, 2011; Matsumoto & Juang, 2013; Shiraev & Levy, 2012). At a more advanced level, there are numerous additional texts with general topical coverage (e.g., van de Vijver, Chasiotis, & Breugelmans, 2011). Texts containing eclectic material on acculturation and adaptation are currently quite popular, with that by Sam and Berry (2016) a prime example. Also, as noted earlier there are now numerous texts that focus on cross-cultural, or multicultural, counseling.

The intent of a recent chapter by Lonner, Keith, & Matsumoto (2018) was to provide a comprehensive compendium of foundations and resources that will be useful in the teaching of cross-cultural psychology. For instance, numerous associations, organizations, and initiatives have become useful resources for psychology instructors or anyone else who wishes to delve into this area. The IACCP (IACCP.org) is obviously a basic resource. It is especially useful because it is the home of the *Online Readings in Psychology and Culture* (ORPC), a free and open access resource mentioned earlier in this Element and specifically founded to be an educational aid.

8 The Past, Present, and Future of Culture and Psychology: Concluding Remarks

A chronology of any scholarly movement obviously has a beginning that, naturally, leads to its present state; together, the past and present portend a future. Culture-oriented psychologists around the world have discussed and debated the chronology of developments in culture and psychology for many years. Most of these discussions took place during dinners or over refreshments.

Some, however, appeared in organized contexts, such as books and sanctioned symposia or panel discussion. For instance, as noted earlier, at the 22nd International IACCP Conference in Reims, France (in 2014) a special symposium was a well-attended feature. I had the pleasure of organizing and chairing an event titled "On the Road to Half a Century of Cross-Cultural Psychology: Foundations, Current Status, and Forecasts." I was fortunate enough to line up a sterling panel of psychologists, all of whom, for roughly half a century, have focused on the interface between psychology and culture. Alphabetically, the participants were John W. Berry (Canada), Pierre R. Dasen (Switzerland and France), Patricia M. Greenfield (the United States), the late Çiğdem Kağıtçıbaşı (Turkey), Ype H. Poortinga (The Netherlands), and Robert Serpell (Zambia). All were generally and similarly familiar with the various approaches in the psychological study of culture, and all spoke about the nature of their involvement in this area and what they thought of all that has transpired for half a century. Their insightful and valuable contributions are instantly available in the *Online Readings on Psychology and Culture,* and are highly recommend.

Greenfield's (2016) presentation in the symposium was titled "Culture in Psychology: Then and Now." She outlined contrasts between 1972 (when the IACCP was founded) and the two-year period of 2013–2014 – nearly half a century later. Greenfield noted four major changes in the past half century. First, in 1972 cross-cultural research in psychology distinctly involved comparisons between two or more cultures, while in recent years other researchers in the Majority World have increasingly been studying their own worlds. Second, there have been major changes in the gender gap. In 1972, culture-oriented research and leadership in psychology was dominated by males, and this imbalance was manifested globally. Incrementally, sharp increases in female researchers, conference attendees, and officers in relevant organizations and associations have essentially wiped out the gender gap. Third, increased mobility and massive globalization, biculturalism, culture-mixing, and migration have had a sizeable influence on the nature of cross-cultural research. In 1972 research on such topics was rather rare, compared with recent trends. Fourth, as Greenfield noted, in 1972 cultures tended to be stable, and the topic of social change did not exist in cross-cultural psychology. Social change, not social stability, is now the rule, and this has altered the nature of cross-cultural research. Greenfield also reminded us, however, that the field of cross-cultural psychology, led by the IACCP, has remained constant over the years with respect to geographic and ethnic diversity. The IACCP and its organizational and leadership structure has been remarkably stable during the past half-century.

I wish to amend Greenfield's comments by noting vast "then and now" differences in how culture-oriented research is conducted and coordinated, how and where it is reported in the psychological literature, and how it is currently taught in universities throughout the world. Technological advances from the "then" days to the present have been stunning. High-speed computers and the Internet have revolutionized every facet of culture-oriented research. In the early days, correspondence was carried on by regular mail, with occasional facsimile (fax) messages speeding things up. I remember feeling rather special when I inherited a used IBM Selectric typewriter. A few years later I felt absolutely noble and privileged when I was allowed to purchase a computer that, along with its "floppy discs," is now a museum piece. Communication via the astonishing World Wide Web (the ubiquitous Internet) is now as common as the air we breathe and is nearly as necessary, if one is to stay in the game. Journal articles in the early days typically had only one or two authors. It is now common to read journal articles with multiple, and sometimes many dozens of authors who can correspond with each other instantly and from almost anywhere. Word-processing programs have revolutionized how books and journal articles are written. The operation of professional journals has seen terrific changes. Books, journals, conferences, and workshops in the area have blossomed like never before. It seems that everyone has "found" culture, and not only in psychology (and of course anthropology). Numerous collateral disciplines feature culture and ethnicity as they carry out their routine activities. Additionally, as reported earlier in this Element psychology education featuring, or at least including, culture has exploded for the better. In short, the highly digitized world ruled by miraculous cyberspace technology has transformed the field, with no end in sight.

I close this Element with some musings and points to ponder. No one knows for certain how many cultures – perhaps more accurately, psycholinguistic groups – there are in the world. Estimates vary over time, and geopolitical circumstances can produce radical changes. Massive emigration and immigration patterns, as well as culture-mixing and the technological advances mentioned earlier have their effects as well (Berry, 2017; Hao, Peng, Peng, & Terrell, 2016). Current estimates of the number of cultures range from 5,000 to 6,000, but that range could depend on how culture is defined. Highly diverse and multiethnic countries such as Canada, the United States, and Russia have hundreds each, and polyglot continents such as Africa and South America have many dozens, if not hundreds, of languages, each defining specific groups or people.

And then there is psychology, the other part of the equation featured in this Element. It is a very interesting, diverse, and fluid profession. For example, the APA currently has 54 divisions. All of them can be congenial to culture-oriented research, especially those that focus on developmental and social psychology. Two divisions, 45 (Society for the Psychological Study of Culture, Ethnicity, and Race) and 52 (International Psychology), are obvious outlets for such research. Both have their own publication outlets (see APA.org). However, the former focuses on US-based diversity and the latter primarily deals with the coordination of international relations (and sponsors an annual award for noteworthy worldwide contributions). The APA's Committee on International Relations in Psychology (CIRP) also sponsors an annual award called Distinguished Contributions to the International Advancement of Psychology. I was honored by receiving awards from Division 52 in 2014 and the CIRP in 2015 (see Lonner, 2015). In recent years a number of cross-cultural psychologists, internationally, have received similar awards.

Additionally, the Association for Psychological Science (APS) attracts culture-oriented research because its base is psychology in the broadest sense. Its main publication, *Psychological Science*, does not focus on culture, but does publish articles consistent with the goals of IACCP (see, for example, Yoo, Miyamoto, Rigotti & Ryff, 2017). The APS also publishes *Perspectives on Psychological Science*; the October 2017 issue featured a special section of invited papers titled "Symposium on Cultural Psychological Science." Symposium participants were psychologists representing both cultural and cross-cultural research. In the United States, Canada, and many other countries, there are many dozens of smaller psychological entities that focus on ethnic groups.

On a broader scale, the International Union of Psychological Science and the International Advancement of Applied Psychology advance and encourage culture-oriented research around the globe, and are supernumerary organizations for many dozens of national and regional psychological associations and societies. Cognitive neuroscientists have recently entered the picture. Such efforts and extensions will continue. If the psychological study of culture lasts another 50 years, it boggles the mind to imagine how it will look. Indeed, it boggles the mind how the entire discipline of psychology will look five decades from now.

So what do we do with this potentially very complex admixture of culture, on one hand, and on the other hand hundreds, if not thousands, of psychological perspectives, theories, and working hypotheses? It would be absurd to think that some gigantic matrix could be developed – something akin to Mendeleyev's Table of Atomic Elements. Hundreds of cultures and ethnic groups have never been touched by inquisitive psychologists. There aren't enough psychologists to cover the globe in the kind of comprehensive and grand fashion that they deserve.

In my opinion there is a rather simple solution to this problem. In the early days of institutionalized cross-cultural psychology, and especially after the JCCP had grown into a stable publication,

I often argued that these efforts de facto have one large purpose or goal: to make themselves obsolete. That would signal "mission accomplished," because the efforts discussed in this Element would have been absorbed, even if only superficially, by everyone in the discipline. Thus, there would no longer be increasingly meaningless divisions such as "cross-cultural" and "cultural" psychology, for they need each other. There would simply be "psychology" writ large. Questions asked, theories applied, and methods used would be fairly uniform, or at least endorsed as reasonable and ethical. The entire research procedure would be – mimicking chemistry or physics – as valid in Istanbul, Caracas, or Tokyo as it would be in Boston, Delhi, or Bangkok. Borrowing the famous line from Shakespeare's *As You Like It*, "All the world is a stage; and all the men and women are mere players." The rest of that passage states that all people and all cultures go through the same stages.

Transposed to the cacophony of cultures and psychological meanderings throughout the world, the bard suggests some sort of uniformity among and between people. In the early days of research in this area, the search for *differences* between different groups was paramount. In recent years, there has been increased interest in searching for *similarities* and even universals.

As anthropologist Donald Brown (1991) noted three decades ago, "given the inherent tendency for disparate peoples to develop disparate cultures, how on earth can some things be the same everywhere?" (p. 88). At some level of abstraction, that observation seems to be eternally true. Most researchers who focus on cultures believe in universals. But they also believe in cultural particulars, whereby universals that are played out on the world stage can vary greatly. I once asked Ernest Boesch why he was involved with cultural psychology and what he wanted his psychologist colleagues to do with it. His answer: No matter what psychologists do and how they do it in their professional work throughout the world, they should never forget that what all people want is their dignity and respect as creative human beings.

I have posited that the thousands of psychologists who, for more than 50 years have studied cultures and how they influence thought and behavior, have established a solid foundation for continued work in this challenging and ever-evolving field. Perhaps the day will come when everything psychologists do accords culture the same level of importance it places on gender and genes. I have often suggested that culture-oriented psychology should assume it has a "death wish" – a wish to no longer be in the fringes and to continue to convince others, successfully, of its importance. If that day comes, thinking cross-culturally will become a central and commonplace component of psychological thinking, research, and application. There would be a grand coalition or unification, and the discipline will be globalized. This has the ring of a happy fairy tale ending, but it could happen earlier than we might think.

References

Aberle, D. F., Cohen, A. K., Davis, A., Levy, M., & Sutton, F. X. (1950). Functional prerequisites of society. *Ethics, 60*, 100–111. doi:10.1086/290705

Adamopoulos, J., & Lonner, W. J. (1994). Absolutism, relativism, and universalism in the study of human behavior. In W. J. Lonner & R. S. Malpass (Eds.), *Psychology and culture* (pp. 129–134). Boston, MA: Allyn & Bacon.

Allik, J., Church, A. T., Ortiz, F. A., Rossier, J., Hrebickova, M., de Fruyt, F., Realo, A.,& McCrae, R. R. (2017). Mean profiles of the NEO Personality Inventory. *Journal of Cross-Cultural Psychology, 48*, 402–420. doi:10.1177 /0022022117692100

Allik, J., & McCrae, R. R. (2004). Toward a geography of personality traits: Patterns of profiles across 36 cultures. *Journal of Cross-Cultural Psychology, 35*, 3–28. doi:10.1177/0022022103260382

Arnett, J. J. (2008). The neglected 95%: Why American psychology needs to become less American. *American Psychologist, 63*, 602–614. doi:10.1037/0003-066X.63.7.602

Berrien, F. K. (1966). Japanese and American values. *International Journal of Psychology, 1*(2), 129–141.

Berrien, F. K. (1967). Methodological and related problems in cross-cultural research. *International Journal of Psychology, 2*(1), 33–43.

Berrien, F. K. (1969). Familiarity, mirror imaging, and social desirability in stereotypes: Japanese vs. Americans. *International Journal of Psychology, 4*(3), 207–215.

Berrien, F. K. (1970). A super-ego for cross-cultural research. *International Journal of Psychology, 5*(1), 33–39.

Berry, J. W. (1969). On cross-cultural comparability. *International Journal of Psychology, 4*, 119–128. doi:10.1080/00207596908247261

Berry, J. W. (1976). *Human ecology and cognitive style: Comparative studies in psychological adaptation.* New York, NY: Sage/Halsted.

Berry, J. W. (2013). Achieving a global psychology. *Canadian Psychology, 24*(3), 55–61. doi:10.103760031246

Berry, J. W. (Ed.) (2017). *Mutual intercultural relations*. New York, NY: Cambridge University Press.

Berry, J. W. (in press). *Oxford intercultural psychology bibliography*. New York, NY: Oxford University Press.

Berry, J. W., Poortinga, Y. H., & Pandey, J. (Eds.) (1997). *Theory and method. Handbook of cross-cultural psychology*, 2nd. edn., vol. 1. Needham Heights, MA:Allyn & Bacon.

Berry, J. W., Poortinga, Y. H, Breugelmans, S. M., Chasiotis, A., & Sam, D. L. (2011). *Cross-cultural psychology: Research and applications*. Cambridge, UK: Cambridge University Press.

Berry, J. W. *et al.* (Eds.) *Handbook of Cross-Cultural Psychology*, 2nd Edition. Rockleigh, MA: Allyn & Bacon.

Boesch, E. E. (1991). *Symbolic action theory*. Berlin, Germany: Springer Verlag.

Boesch, E. E. (1996). The seven flaws of cross-cultural psychology: The story of a conversion. *Mind, Culture, and Activity, 3*(1), 2-10. doi:10.1207/s15327884mca0301_2

Bond, M. H. (Ed.) (2015). *Working at the interface of cultures: Eighteen lives in social science (psychology revivals)*. New York, NY: Routledge.

Brislin, R. W. (1970). Back translation for cross-cultural research. *Journal of Cross-Cultural Psychology, 1*, 185-216.

Brislin, R. W., Bochner, S., & Lonner, W. J. (Eds.) (1975). *Cross-cultural perspectives on Learning*. New York, NY: Sage/Halsted.

Brislin, R. W., Lonner, W. J., & Thorndike, R. M. (1973). *Cross-cultural research methods*. New York, NY: Wiley-Interscience.

Brown, D. E. (1991). *Human universals*. Philadelphia, PA: Temple University Press.

Campbell, D. T., & Naroll, R. (1972). The mutual methodological relevance of anthropology and psychology. In F. L. K. Hsu (Ed.), *Psychological anthropology* (rev. edn.; pp. 435-563). Cambridge, MA: Schenkman.

Chinese Culture Connection. (1987). Chinese values and the search for culture-free dimensions of culture. *Journal of Cross-Cultural Psychology, 18*, 143-174.

Cole, M. (1984). The world beyond our borders: What might our students need to know about it? *American Psychologist, 39*, 998-1005. doi:10.1037/0003-066X.39.9.998

Cole, M. (2006). *Cultural psychology: A once and future discipline*. Cambridge, MA: Belknap/Harvard.

Cronbach, L. J., & Drenth, P. J. D. (Eds.) (1972). *Mental tests and cultural adaptation.* The Hague: Mouton.

Dawson, J. L. W., & Lonner, W. J. (Eds.) (1974). *Readings in cross-cultural psychology.* Hong Kong, China: Hong Kong University Press.

de Raad, B., Barelds, D., Zimmerman, M., de Roover, K., Mlačić, B., & Church, A. T. (2014). Towards a pan-cultural personality structure: Input from 11 Psycholexical studies. *European Journal of Personality, 28*, 497–510. doi:10.1002/per.1953

Fischer, R., & Poortinga, Y. H. (Eds.) (in press). Reflections on methodology and theory in cross-cultural psychology. *Journal of Cross-Cultural Psychology.*

Fischer, R., & Poortinga, Y. H. (Eds.) (in press). Contemporary culture-comparative research: What is worrisome and how can we do better? In R. Fischer & Y. H. Poortinga (Eds.) Reflections on methodology and theory in cross-cultural psychology. *Journal of Cross-Cultural Psychology.*

Fontaine, J. R. J. (2011). A fourfold conceptual framework for cultural and cross-cultural: relativism, construct universalism, repertoire universalism, and absolutism. In F. J. R. van de Vijver, A. Chasiotis, & S. M. Breugelmans (Eds.), *Fundamental questions in cross cultural psychology* (pp. 165–189). Cambridge, UK: Cambridge University Press.

Frijda, N., & Jahoda, G. (1966). On the scope and methods of cross-cultural research. *International Journal of Psychology, 1*(2), 109–127. doi:10.1080/00207596608247118

Fuentes, M. A., & Shannon, C. R. (2016). The state of multiculturalism and diversity in undergraduate psychological training. *Teaching of Psychology, 43*, 197–203. doi:10.1177/009862

Geertz, C. (1973). *The interpretation of cultures.* New York, NY: Basic Books.

Gerstein, L. H., Heppner, P. P., Aegisdottir, S., Leung, S.-M. A., & Norsworthy, K. L. (2009). *International handbook of cross-cultural counseling: Cultural assumptions and practices worldwide.* Thousand Oaks, CA: Sage.

Gold, M. (1999). *The complete social scientist: A Kurt Lewin reader.* Washington, DC: American Psychological Association.

Greenfield, P. M. (2000). Three approaches to the psychology of culture: Where do they come from? Where can they go? *Asian Journal of Social Psychology, 3*, 223–240. doi:10.1111/1467-839X.00066

Greenfield, P. M. (2016). *Culture in psychology: Then and now.* In C. Roland-Lévy, P. Denoux, B. Voyer, P. Boski, & W. K. Gabrenya Jr. (Eds.), *Unity, diversity and culture: Research and scholarship selected from the 22nd Congress of the International Association for Cross-Cultural Psychology.* Melbourne, FL: International Association for Cross-Cultural Psychology. Accessed via www.iaccp.org.

Griggs. R. A., & Jackson, S. L. (2013). Introductory psychology textbooks: An objective analysis update. *Teaching of Psychology, 40,* 163–168. doi:10.1177/00986283134877455

Hao, J., Li, D., Peng, L., Peng, S., & Torelli, C. J. (2016). Special issue: Cultural mixing, its nature and psychological implications. *Journal of Cross-Cultural Psychology, 47.* doi:10.1177/0022022116670514

Heine, S. (2012). *Cultural psychology* (2nd edn.). New York, NY: Norton.

Henrich, J., Heine, S., & Norenzayan, A. (2010). The weirdest people in the world? *Behavioral and Brain Sciences, 33,* 6183. doi:10.1017/S01405225X0999152X

Hofstede, G. (1980). *Culture's consequences: International differences in work-related values.* Beverly Hills, CA: Sage.

Hofstede, G. (2001). *Culture's consequences: Comparing values, behaviors, institutions, and organizations across cultures.* Thousand Oaks, CA: Sage.

Hsu, F. L. K. (Ed.) (1972). *Psychological anthropology* (rev. edn.). Cambridge,MA: Schenkman.

Jahoda, G. (1970). A cross-cultural perspective in psychology. *Advancement of Science, 27,* 1–4. [Presidential address delivered to Section J (Psychology) on September 4, 1970, at the Durham Meeting of the British Association.]

Jahoda, G. (1982). *Psychology and anthropology: A psychological perspective.* London,UK: Academic Press.

Jahoda, G. (1992). *Crossroads between culture and mind.* New York, NY: Harvester Wheatsheaf.

Jahoda, G. (2011). Past and present of cross-cultural psychology. In F. J. R. van de Vijver, A. Chasiotis, & S. M. Breugelmans (Eds.), *Fundamental questions in cross-cultural psychology* (pp. 37–63). Cambridge, UK: Cambridge University Press.

Jahoda, G., & Krewer, B. (1997). History of cross-cultural and cultural psychology. In J. W. Berry, Y. H. Poortinga, & J. Pandey (Eds.), *Handbook of cross-cultural psychology Vol. 1. Theory and method* (pp. 1–42). Boston, MA: Allyn & Bacon.

Kağıtçıbaşı, C. (1997). Individualism and collectivism. In J. W. Berry, M. H. Segall, & C. Kağıtçıbaşı (Eds.), *Handbook of cross-cultural psychology, Vol. III, Social behavior and applications* (pp. 1–49). Boston, MA: Allyn & Bacon.

Keith, K. D. (2012). The culture of teaching and the teaching of culture. *Psychology Learning and Teaching, 11,* 316–325. doi:10.2304/plat.2012.11.3.316

Keith, K. D. (Ed.). (2013). *The encyclopedia of cross-cultural psychology, Vols. 1–3.* Chichester, UK: Wiley-Blackwell.

Keith, K. D. (Ed.). (2018). *Culture across the curriculum: A psychology teacher's handbook.* Cambridge, UK: Cambridge University Press.

Kim, U. (1995). Psychology, science and culture: Cross-cultural analyses of national psychologies in developing countries. *International Journal of Psychology, 30,* 663–679. doi:10.1080/00207599508246593

Kim, U., Park, Y.-S., & Park, D. (2000). The challenge of cross-cultural psychology: The role of indigenous psychologies. *Journal of Cross-Cultural Psychology, 31,* 63–79. doi:10.1177/0022022100031001006

Klineberg, O. (1980). Perspectives on cross-cultural psychology before 1960. In H. C. Triandis & W. W. Lambert (Eds.), *Handbook of cross-cultural psychology, Vol. 1, Perspectives.* Boston, MA: Allyn & Bacon.

Laungani, P. D. (2007). *Understanding cross-cultural psychology: Eastern and western perspectives.* London, UK: Sage.

Leong, F. L. T. (Ed.) *The APA handbook of multicultural psychology, Vol. 1, Theory and Research.* Washington, DC: American Psychological Association.

Leung, K., & Bond, M. H. (Eds.) (2010). *Psychological aspects of social axioms.* New York, NY: Springer Science & Business Media.

Lewin, K. (1936). *Principles of topological psychology.* New York, NY: McGraw-Hill.

Lewin, K., & Gold, M. (1999). *The complete social scientist: A Kurt Lewin reader.* Washington, DC: American Psychological Association.

Lonner, W. J. (1968). The SVIB visits German, Austrian and Swiss psychologists. *American Psychologist, 23,* 164–179.

Lonner, W. J. (1975). An analysis of the prepublication evaluation of cross-cultural manuscripts: Implications for future research. In R. W. Brislin, S., Bochner, & W. J. Lonner (Eds.), *Cross-cultural perspectives on learning* (pp. 305–320). New York, NY: Halstead Press.

Lonner, W. J. (1980). The search for psychological universals. In H. C. Triandis & W. W. Lambert (Eds.), *Handbook of cross cultural psychology, vol. 1* (pp. 143–204). Boston, MA: Allyn & Bacon.

Lonner, W. J. (1989). The introductory psychology text and cross-cultural psychology: Beyond Ekman, Whorf and biased I.Q. tests. In D. Keats, D. Munro, & L. Mann (Eds.), *Heterogeneity in cross-cultural psychology* (pp. 4–22). Lisse, The Netherlands: Swets & Zeitlinger.

Lonner, W. J. (2011). The continuing challenge of finding "order" across cultures. In F. J. R. van de Vijver, A. Chasiotis, & S. M. Breugelmans (Eds.), *Fundamental questions in cross-cultural psychology* (pp. 64–94). Cambridge, UK: Cambridge University Press.

Lonner, W. J. (2013). Foreword. In K. D. Keith (Ed.), *The encyclopedia of cross-cultural psychology, Vol. 1* (pp. xl–li). Chichester, UK: Wiley-Blackwell. [Also published in *Online Readings in Psychology and Culture* as *Chronological benchmarks in cross-cultural psychology: Foreword to the encyclopedia of cross-cultural psychology*, http://scholarworks.gvsu.edu/orpc/vol1/iss2/1/].

Lonner, W. J. (2015). Half a century of cross-cultural psychology: A grateful coda. *American Psychologist, 70*, 804–814. doi:10.1037/a0039454

Lonner, W. J. (2016). On the road to half a century of cross-cultural psychology: Foundations, current status, and forecasts. In C. Roland-Lévy, P. Denoux, B. Voyer, P. Boski, & W. K. Gabrenya Jr. (Eds.), *Unity, diversity and culture* (pp. 10–11). Melbourne, FL: International Association for Cross-Cultural Psychology. Accessed via www.iaccp.org.

Lonner, W. J., & Adamopoulos, J. (1997). *Culture as antecedent to behavior.* In J. W. Berry, Y. H. Poortinga, & J. Pandey (Eds.), *Handbook of cross-cultural psychology: Vol. 1 Theory and method* (pp. 43–83). Boston, MA: Allyn & Bacon.

Lonner, W. J., & Berry, J. W. (Eds.) (1986). *Field methods in cross-cultural research.* Beverly Hills, CA:Sage.

Lonner, W. J., Dinnel, D. L., Forgays, D. K., & Hayes, S. A. (Eds.) (1999). Merging past, present, and future in cross-cultural psychology. *Selected papers from the fourteenth international congress of the International Association for Cross-Cultural Psychology.* Lisse, The Netherlands: Swets & Zeitlinger.

Lonner, W. J., & Hayes, S. A. (Eds.) (2007). *Discovering cultural psychology: A profile and selected readings of Ernest E. Boesch.* Charlotte, NC: Information Age Publishing.

Lonner, W. J., Keith, K. D., & Matsumoto, D. (in press). Culture and the psychology curriculum: Foundations and resources. In D. Matsumoto & H.-C. Hwang (Eds.), *The Oxford handbook of culture and psychology.* New York, NY: Oxford University Press.

Lonner, W. J., & Malpass, R. S. (Eds.), *Psychology and culture* (pp. 129-134). Boston, MA: Allyn & Bacon.

Lonner, W. J., & Murdock, E. (2008). *Introductory psychology texts and the inclusion of culture. Online Readings in Psychology and Culture.* Unit 11.1. Retrieved from: http://scholarworks.gvsu.edu/orpc/vol11/iss1/1/.

Markus, H. R., & Kitayama, S. (1991). Culture and the self: Implications for cognition, emotion, and motivation. *Psychological Review, 98,* 224-253. doi:10.1037/0033-295X.98.2.224

Matsumoto, D. (Ed.) (2001). *The handbook of culture and psychology.* Oxford, UK: Oxford University Press.

Matsumoto, D., & Hwang, H.-C. (Eds.) (in press) *The Oxford handbook of culture and psychology.* New York, NY: Oxford University Press.

Matsumoto, D., & Juang, L. (2013). *Culture and psychology* (5th edn.). Belmont, CA: Wadsworth.

Matsumoto, D., & van de Vijver, F. J. R. (Eds.) (2011). *Cross cultural research methods in psychology.* New York, NY: Cambridge University Press.

Matsumoto, D., & Yoo, S, H. (2006). Toward a new generation of cross-cultural research. *Perspectives on Psychological Science, 1,* 234-250. doi:10.1111/j.1745-6916.2006.00014.x

McCrae, R. R., Terracciano, A., & 78 members of the Personality Profiles of Cultures Project. (2005). Universal features of personality traits from the observer's perspective. Data from 50 cultures. *Journal of Personality and Social Psychology, 88,* 547-561. doi:10.1037/0022-3514.88.3.547

Miller, B., & Gentile, B. F. (1998). Introductory course content and goals. *Teaching of Psychology, 25,* 89-96. doi:10.1207/s15328023top2502

Miller, G. A. (1969). Psychology as a means of promoting human welfare. *American Psychologist, 24,* 1076-1092.

Morris, M. W., Chiu, C.-y. & Liu, Z. (2015). Polycultural psychology. *Annual Review of Psychology, 66,* 631–659. doi:10.1146/annurev-psych-0108114-015001

Myers, D. G., & DeWall, C. N. (2015). *Psychology* (11th edn.). New York, NY: Worth.

Nisbett, R. E. (2003). *The geography of thought: How Asians and Westerners think differently and why.* New York, NY: The Free Press.

Norenzayan, A., & Heine, S. J. (2005). Psychological universals: What are they and how can we know? *Psychological Bulletin, 131,* 763–784. doi:10.1037/0033-2909.131.5.763

Pedersen, P., Lonner, W. J., & Draguns, J. G. (1976). *Counseling across cultures.* Honolulu, HI: East-West Center.

Pedersen, P. B., Lonner, W. J., Draguns, J. G., Trimble, J. E., & del Rio, M. S. (2015). *Counseling across cultures* (7th edn.). Thousand Oaks, CA Sage Publications.

Pike, K. (1967). *Language in relation to a unified theory of the structure of human behaviour* (2nd edn.). The Hague, Netherlands: Mouton.

Richmond, A. S., Broussard, K. A., Sterns, J. L., Sanders, K. K., & Shardy, J. C. (2015). Who are we studying? Sample diversity in teaching of psychological research, *Teaching of Psychology, 42,* 218–226. doi:10.1177/0098628315587619

Rivers, W. H. R. (1901). Introduction and vision. In A. C. Haddon (Ed.), *Reports of the Cambridge anthropological expedition to the Torres Straits, Vol. 2, Pt. 1.* Cambridge, UK: Cambridge University Press.

Roland-Lévy, C., Denoux, P., Voyer, B., Boski, P., & Gabrenya, Jr., W. K. (Eds.) (2016). *Unity, diversity and culture: Research and scholarship selected from the 22nd Congress of the International Association for Cross-Cultural Psychology.* Melbourne, Florida, USA: International Association for Cross-Cultural Psychology. Accessed via www.iaccp.org.

Sam, D. L., & Berry, J. W. (Eds.) (2016). *The Cambridge handbook of acculturation psychology.* Cambridge, UK: Cambridge University Press.

Sam, D. L. & Berry, J. W. (Eds.) (2017). *Cross-cultural psychology, Vols. 1–4.* New York, NY: Routledge.

Schwartz, S. S. (1992). An overview of the Schwartz theory of human values. In *Online Readings in Psychology and Culture,* Unit 2.1. Retrieved from: http://scholarworks.gvsu.edu/orpc/vol2/iss1/11/

Schwartz, S. (2006). A theory of cultural value orientations: Explication and implications. *Comparative Sociology, 5,* 136–182. doi:10.1163/156913306778667357.

Scott, C., & Safdar, S. (2016). The inclusion of culture in Canadian social psychology textbooks: A content analysis of introductory textbooks. *Online Readings in Psychology and Culture* Unit 11. Retrieved from: http://scholarworks.gvsu.edu/orpc/vol11/iss1/2/.

Segall, M. H. (1979). *Cross-cultural psychology: Human behavior in global perspective.* Monterey, CA: Brooks-Cole.

Segall, M. H., Lonner, W. J., & Berry, J. W. (1998). Cross-cultural psychology as a scholarly discipline: On the flowering of culture in behavioral research. *American Psychologist, 53,* 1101–1110. doi:10.1037/0003-066X.53.10.1101

Shweder, R., & Sullivan, M. (1993). Cultural psychology – who needs it? *Annual Review of Psychology, 44,* 497–523. doi:10.1146/annurev.ps.44.020193.002433

Shiraev, E. B., & Levy, D. (2012). *Cross-cultural psychology: Critical thinking and Contemporary applications* (5th edn.). New York, NY: Pearson.

Smith, P. B., & Best, D. L. (Eds.) (2009). *Cross-cultural psychology. Vols. 1–4.* Thousand Oaks, CA: Sage.

Spreen, O., & Spreen, G. (1963). The MMPI in a German-speaking population: Standardization report and methodological problems of cross-cultural interpretations. *Acta Psychologica, 21,* 265–273.

Takooshian, H., Gielen, U. P., Plous, S., Rich, G. J., & Velayo, R. S. (2016). Internationalizing undergraduate psychology education: Trends, techniques, and technologies. *American Psychologist, 72,* 136–147. doi:10.1037/a0039977

Triandis, H. C. (1972). *The analysis of subjective culture.* New York, NY: John Wiley and Sons.

Triandis, H. C. (1995). *Individualism and collectivism.* Boulder, CO: Westview Press.

Triandis, H. C., & Berry, J. W. (Eds.) (1980). *Handbook of cross-cultural psychology, Vol. 2, Methodology.* Rockleigh, NJ: Allyn & Bacon.

Triandis, H. C., Berry. J. W., Brislin, R. W., Draguns, J. D., Heron, A., & Lonner. W. J. (Eds.)(1980). *Handbook of cross-cultural psychology, Vols. 1–6.* Rockleigh, NJ: Allyn & Bacon.

Triandis, H. C., & Brislin, R. W. (1984). Cross-cultural psychology. *American Psychologist, 38,*10061016. doi:10.1037/0003-066X.39.9.1006

Valsiner, J. (2007). *Culture in minds and societies: Foundations of cultural psychology.* Los Angeles, CA: Sage.

Valsiner, J. (2009). Cultural psychology today: Innovations and oversights. *Culture & Psychology, 15,* 5–39. doi:10.1177/1354067X08101427

van de Vijver, F. J. R., Chasiotis, A., & Breugelmans, S. M. (Eds.) (2011). *Fundamental questions in cross-cultural psychology.* Cambridge, UK: Cambridge University Press.

van de Vijver, F. J. R., & Leung, K. (1997) *Methods and data analysis in cross-cultural research.* Thousand Oaks, CA: Sage.

Warwick, D. P. (1980). The politics and ethics of cross-cultural research. In H. C. Triandis & W. Lambert (Eds.), *Handbook of cross-cultural psychology, Vol. 1, Perspectives.* Boston, MA: Allyn & Bacon.

Wesley, F., & Karr, C. (1966). Problems in establishing norms for cross-cultural comparisons. *International Journal of Psychology, 1,* 257–262.

Wrenn, C. G. (1962). The culturally encapsulated counselor. *Harvard Educational Review, 32,* 444–449.

Wundt, W. (1900–1920). *Volkerpsychologie (Vols. 1–10). Leipzig, Germany: Engelmann.[Elements of folk psychology.* London, UK: Allen & Unwin.

Yoo, J., Miyamoto, Risotto, A., & Ryff (2017). Linking positive affect to blood lipids: A cultural perspective. *Psychological Science, 28,* 1468–1477. http://doi.org/10.1177/0956797617713309

Cambridge Elements ⹀

Psychology and Culture

Kenneth D. Keith

University of San Diego

Kenneth D. Keith is author or editor of more than 160 publications on cross-cultural psychology, quality of life, intellectual disability, and the teaching of psychology. He was the 2017 president of the Society for the Teaching of Psychology.

About the series

Elements of Psychology and Culture will feature authoritative surveys and updates on key topics in cultural, cross-cultural, and indigenous psychology. Authors are internationally recognized scholars whose work is at the forefront of their subdisciplines within the realm of psychology and culture.

Cambridge Elements ≡
Psychology and Culture

Elements in the series

The Continuing Growth of Cross-Cultural Psychology: A First-Person Annotated Chronology
Walter J. Lonner
9781108461726

A full series listing is available at: www.cambridge.org/EPAC

Printed in the United States
By Bookmasters